Angelic Files

Michael Aviel

Pulpit to Page Publishing Co. books may be ordered through booksellers or by contacting:

Pulpit to Page Publishing Co.
Warsaw, Indiana
pulpittopage.com

ISBN: 978-1986161442
ISBN: 1986161447

Library of Congress Control Number: 2018936808

DEDICATION

It is with a full heart and thankful heart that I want to first and foremost, dedicate this book to my King, my best friend and brother, the Lord Jesus Christ. He has been incredible and so gracious to me throughout this most challenging and exciting journey of writing my first book.

I am truly grateful to so many of you who have helped to read, edit, critique, advise and affirm. Your help has been invaluable and I want to say, *thank you so very much.*

This book is also dedicated to all those who are passionate lovers of Jesus Christ and who are willing to embrace all of what our Heavenly Father has made available to us as citizens of the Kingdom of Heaven.

I dedicate this book to the sons of God.

Endorsements

The book "Angelic Files", is essential reading for anyone who wants to learn about the mystical realm of angels. The subject is approached in a fresh, systematic, orderly in-depth with rare personal encounters from the abundance of Michael's fellowship with the Lord.
Read this book if you feel a leading to learn more about angels, or if you are having experiences that you need to understand more. I highly recommend it!

— Gabriel James Dziya
Supernatural Encounters With Gabriel James Dziya.
The Angel With The Lion's Head (Anthology Of Heavenly Visions).
smashwords.com/profile/view/GabrielDziya
facebook.com/james.dziya

Angelic files is a simple yet incisive instructional manual that details the clusters of Angels nests, their functionality and intended partnership with the Church in these last days. Combining personal encounters and scriptural illumination, Michael has been graced to bring understanding to the emerging mystical company that is arising across all the nations of the earth. He is among a rare breed of pure yet integral leaders in the earth emerging today in terms of Apostolic leadership that are spearheading the ingathering of leaders from the world who will be used by the Lord to bring in the final harvest and the finalization of the ultimate purposes of God for this generation. Get ready to have your spiritual taste buds appetized and sumptuously fed with the finest of Zion's feasts, truly the Lord has reserved His finest wine for the last hour.

— Steve Kioko
House of David
facebook.com/steve.kioko.332
Kenya

CONTENTS

Forward

I remember hearing a sermon some years ago about Moses. The speaker was the late prophet Art Katz and, as usual, his perspective on Moses was something I had never before considered. It centered on the burning bush, or more precisely, on Moses' response to the burning bush. As it happened, Moses was confronted with a supernatural moment and decided it was worth looking at. The scriptures say that Moses decided to "turn aside to see this great sight." And, it was only after Moses "turned aside to see" that the Lord called his name and initiated Moses' earthly and supernatural ministry.

Art Katz took great care to emphasize how important it was to stop in your tracks, cease what you are doing, and turn aside your life to embrace something unprecedented. And now, I would like to extend that same emphasis to you, the reader, concerning this book. For that is exactly what Michael Aviel has done, and it's what we all need to do, as well.

Michael is one of a growing number of people who dare to stop in their current path and turn aside to see what has never been seen before. And we should make no mistake about it, you have to stop what you are doing to "turn aside and see." Any book about angels and the magnificent access we have to the heavenly realms – the very power to see those angels and interact with them – will require a stoppage of your normal routine and the discipline and patience to turn aside and gaze on something wondrous.

But it's worth your focus, and *Angelic Files* does a great job of showing us why. At every stage in his journey, Michael is always pointing to the source of our access to the angels – Jesus the Messiah. If you dare to open your life to this kind of experience, I have no doubt that your love for God will grow and blossom as it did with Michael. It will draw you up into the loving arms of the Lord, and that is the safest place to begin an actual relationship with the angelic world.

There are a lot of books that talk *about* the angels, but not many that talk *with* the angels. *Angelic Files* chronicles Michael's journey to befriend the angels just as Jesus directed, and I've often thought that one of the defining traits of an authentic angelic encounter was the value and desire for real relationship. In every angelic conversation that Michael has recorded, we're invited to do the same. We're offered an access that goes beyond seeing what the angels can do for us, to asking how Jesus' love can be demonstrated in a sincere friendship with them. In a world that seems to use things (and people) according to what they can provide, Michael Aviel takes the most important leap of entering into a relationship based on Christ's selfless love.

If we take just a casual look at biblical and spiritual history, we can see that this is the direction God has been leading humanity for millennia. We have been on a slow but steady march of angelic discovery. And, in every age, the relationship improves. *Angelic Files* is one more piece of the puzzle that we all need to keep moving forward in the Christ-centered angelic interaction.

– Christopher Paul Carter
Author of *Caught Up in the Spirit, In the Palaces of Heaven, and Cosmic Shift*
discovertheheavens.org/

Preface

And the angel of the Lord said unto him, Why askest thou thus after my name, seeing it is secret? (Judges 13:18)

The secret things belong to God, yet He Himself *is* the secret that awaits our discovery. Herein lies a deep mystical truth which I believe is an antidote to all our fears of engaging with the unknown.

The Father in His kindness has generously veiled Himself within the Son. The Son is the revelation of the beauty of the Father and His Kingdom. Hence, the Son is the illumination of the hidden things of the Father, the uncovering of the thick darkness around His throne (1 Kings 8:12), and the whisperer of all Kingdom secrets. The Oxford dictionary defines the word 'secret' as something that is kept or meant to be kept unknown or unseen by others. With that in mind, I am compelled to re-examine the angel's response to Manoah, *"Why askest thou thus after my name, seeing it is secret?" (Judges 13:18)*

In what manner is the name of the Angel of the Lord a secret? Is it indirectly insinuating that mankind is prohibited from asking the names of angels? If we look carefully, we will see that an invitation is hidden within this angel's response. Kingdom secrets are an invitation to friendship. Friendship with the Son is a key that unlocks the door to mysteries.

Manoah was not just asking the angel for his name; he was really enquiring about the nature and character of the angel. The angel was inviting Manoah to be mystically acquainted with him, and in doing so, discover the nature of the angel.

The Son Jesus Christ is the mystic secret of God, and He (Jesus) unveils every facet of the Kingdom in His glorious face. The angelic canopy is a facet of the Kingdom that awaits our discovery and the same question is posed to us by them, *"Why askest thou thus after our nature, seeing it is secret?"*

Introduction

Throughout history, angels have long been the topic of intrigue and awe. Who are these mysterious and magnificent beings? How many of them did God create? Are they good and/or bad? Can we interact with them? Do they have names? Do I have a personal angel? Can I see them? Can I talk with them? And the list goes on.

The Bible is filled with numerous encounters and visitations of angels with mankind. There are the Seraphim, the Cherubim, the four living creatures, and the angels of the Lord. But if we look more carefully, hidden and apparently nameless, except for their function and mandate, we see that there are angels who look like us. There are angels who war on our behalf, who protect, who bring messages, who are scribes, who place marks upon people, who bring laws, and so much more.

The scriptures tell us that there are ten thousand times ten thousands of angels that encircle the throne of YHVH, crying out with loud voices in worship to the Lord. This structure of encircling that we see in the throne room of YHVH is the structure that will fully surround a mature son of God.

According to some ancient biblical writings, there is a nine-layered angelic canopy. Each layer has a general or a sentient angel that is its leader. Within this multi-layered angelic canopy, there are unknown angels yet to be discovered. Some of these are guardian angels, and these angels have a strong "parent" angel. The parent angel is the angel that oversees the guardian angel.

There are always angels around us, but we have been mostly unaware of them and the charge that they have been given in our lives. My goal in writing this book is to outline to you some biblical and revelatory truths that can trigger angelic manifestations and enable you to begin to interact with the angels. As sons of God and citizens of heaven, we have full access to interact with the angelic canopy. But before we dive into the vast files of the angels, let us deal with a precursor to angelic interaction, which is *sight*.

Seeing Through the Lens of the Scriptures

We have all heard that those who are able to see in the spirit have been specially gifted to do so, and while that may be true, I believe that seeing is an inheritance of all sons of YHVH and can enable us to live more fully as new creation beings.

Seeing actually brings our entire being into the conscious reality of the Kingdom realms of our Father where we can encounter and engage with the inhabitants of heaven. This changes the dynamics of how we function as we begin to live from heaven to earth instead of from earth hoping for heaven.

For us to be able to engage with the angels, we should be able to see, sense, perceive, know, and feel, which in the spirit is sight, as all our senses converge in the realm of the spirit. I call this 'knowing,' for our entire being has the capacity to 'see.' However, this would take the exercise or the practice of our spiritual senses. This exercise involves the discovery of the different avenues of our spirit man. These avenues enable our spirit man to relate to the spiritual world.

"But strong meat belongeth to them that are of full age, even those who by reason of use have their senses exercised to discern both good and evil." (Hebrews 5:8)

A place for the practical activation of our sight is to see into the Word of God. The scriptures should be our plumbline and the foundation for all our engagements as it is full of _word pictures_ that can help to activate our spiritual eyes. Insight into the scriptures (which is the revelation of the living Word, Jesus Christ) is a launch pad for seeing into the realm of the spirit.

Not too long ago, I had a night vision where I found myself reading what seemed to be an extensive version of the book of Matthew. I was surprised and shocked to find that there was an 'extensive version' and I tried to check what version of the Bible I was reading. Immediately, I was sucked into the crucifixion scene and I saw the scarred, bruised body of Jesus being lowered onto a rocky place. The edges of the rocks were cutting into His body as they laid Him from the cross to the ground. I saw how the Jews who had cried "crucify

Him" spat upon the ground in scorn and disgust. He laid there like an insult to Israel, "King of the Jews." I saw how the Romans soldiers looked mockingly at His corpse. As His pure, innocent blood drained from His mutilated body to the ground, men in white linen stood afar off in mid-air, weeping in horror at the price that the Son of God had paid. There was a sense of deep abandonment that our Lord experienced on the cross. Even though John, Jesus' mother, and various other women stood at the cross, our King was alone. The place was fraught with a deep sense of loneliness. The atmosphere surrounding Him was thick with darkness and pulsated with deep rejection. This was my rejected King.

I saw that the moment He breathed His last breath, His Spirit moved throughout Israel seeking for those who were mourning for the crucified King, to mark their hearts to be receptive to the Kingdom of God when the dispensation of the Holy Spirit was to begin. What Yeshua had accomplished on the cross had elevated humanity into the domain and realm of relationally interacting with high angelic beings.

The Scriptures hold within their pages an invitation for us to come and look into the dimensions and depths of the experiential Christ. From a place of intimacy with Jesus, we are drawn into the very life of the scriptures. It is the living Word of God who has framed the spiritual universes, and every aspect and encounter in the realms of the spirit is to continuously reveal the Christ.

Let us journey together into the voice of the scriptures concerning our relationship with angels. The presence of the Lord Jesus Christ is key to our engagement with the angels, as He is the one who fitly knits everything together. Everything is from Him, through Him, and to Him.

Throughout this book, you will read about the Kingdom of God, love, faith, Mount Zion, and much more. Interwoven within all of this is the ONE, the desire above all desires, my beloved Yeshua. I cannot truly write about the angels, about encounters or visitations, without writing about Him who is the reason for it all.

My desire is to share with you some of the files of the angels within the scriptures and what has been revealed to me through my encounters and visitations with them. Get a cup of coffee; get your preferred device for journaling, and let us sit with the Lord as I invite you to journey with me into the *Angelic Files*.

I assume that we have our cups of coffee ready; I prefer tea. Let us look at some foundational truths concerning our relationship with the angels in the Kingdom of heaven.

Chapter 1

Angels, Prayer, Worship

'Behold, are they not all spirits of service, who are sent into service for the sake of those who are going to inherit life?" (Hebrews 1:14, Aramaic Version)

For too long, we have shied away from the topic of angels, and it seems as if it were more natural for us to be aware of the demonic realm and how it functions rather than the angelic realm. If we begin to see from heaven's perspective, that angels are spirits in the service of the Lord, we will not be afraid to interact with them for fear of being deceived by false angels. If our belief system revolves around fear, then we are missing out on some of the most precious gifts that YHVH has made available to His children.

When a reference to angels is made, the first thing that comes to mind is a *'winged messenger,'* who is *only* there to protect us but with whom we are not allowed to know or to engage with. Our misconception of their true identity has held us back from interacting with them. Yes, angels are messengers, but they are more than that.

To our God and King, angels are spirits employed in His service. Jesus Christ, our servant Bridegroom King, has purposed to manifest His service to humanity through these spirit beings we call angels. They are the manifestation of His servitude aspect. As our Lord Jesus Christ Himself said,

"For the Son of man came not to be ministered unto but to minister." (Matthew 20:28)

The truth is that the word 'angels' does not adequately describe them. Thomas Aquinas puts it well:

"The word 'angel' does not properly describe their nature; it only describes what they do in relationship to us. Angels are more properly referred to as "spirits," for this is who they are."

One day, I was praying and asking YHVH to release the spirit of excellence upon me as I had a task that I had to do. Immediately, the Lord motioned me to directly speak with an angel of excellence, as the *spirit of excellence* is also the *angel of excellence*. Like always, I quieted myself and asked the Holy Spirit, the infuser and energizer of all spirits, to grant me angelic tongues to interact with the angel of excellence.

Many of us have prayed and asked for different impartations of the spirit(s) of God: spirit of prosperity, spirit of deliverance, spirit of wisdom, spirit of strength, and so on.

Does this mean that these are all different manifestations of the Holy Spirit? Yes and no. Every being in heaven is first classified as a spirit, as its identity is found within the nature of its spirit. For example, we are mostly comfortable with saying that the angel of breakthrough is here, rather than referring to him in accordance to his rightful nature, which is a spirit of breakthrough. Oftentimes, when we say the 'spirit of breakthrough,' the majority of us think that this is the Holy Spirit because of the term 'spirit.' We need to continuously remember that angels are spirits.

The Holy Spirit is the Spirit of the Living Christ, the essence of Jesus that infuses and makes His abode in us. He is the Spirit of sonship and He has 'spirits' under Him, whom we call angels, but remember their true classification are spirits, just as we are. So we should really identify an *angel* of deliverance as the *spirit* of deliverance. What differentiates him from other spirits (angels) is that the light spectrums of the Holy Spirit that infuse his service are those of YHVH, the mighty Deliverer. The Holy Spirit gives him (the angel) his identity.

Notice how Paul prays for the spirit of wisdom and revelation to be given to the Ephesians. In other versions, the spirit is referred to as '*a spirit of wisdom and revelation*' (Ephesians 1:17, Berea Study Bible, New American Standard Version, Holman Christian Bible).

This completely changes our perspective. Try reading Ephesians 1:17 like this: *"May the God of our Lord Jesus Christ, the glorious Father, give you an angel of wisdom and revelation in your knowledge of Him."*

We should start seeing the angels as spirits of a high order who are assigned to be of service. They are spirits of service, not just mere messengers. We are spirit beings, as well. Should it not be the natural inclination for spirits born of the light of Christ to interact with spirits that bring His light of servitude? If that was not the case, for what reason would the Holy Spirit give us tongues of angels, if not to communicate with the angels (1 Corinthians 13:1)? Or bring us to Mount Zion, to an innumerable company of angels (Hebrews 12:22)?

Who am I "praying" to?

"How close to us stands one of the celestial spirits (angel), who from the cradle to the grave never leaves us for an instant. He guides us, he protects us like a friend, like a brother. This should be a source of constant consolation for us, especially during the saddest times of our lives." (Padre Pios)

So, I conversed with the angel, and the angel conversed with me. I had dialogued with a celestial being. Was I treading on shaky grounds? Had the angel begun to slowly take the place of my beautiful Yeshua? Was it legal to commune with an angel, or rather should I say *'pray'* to an angel? Did not my theological mindset and religious upbringing define prayer as, 'talking to God' and should be reserved for God and God alone? Did my desire for engaging the angelic canopy take me beyond the boundary line of error and truth? "Jesus! I am afraid," I pleaded. "If I converse with the angels, Lord, am I praying to them?"

Our misconception of prayer, as YHVH defines it, has held us back from interacting with angels. At large, we have narrowed prayer to just verbally talking with God, which is true. But prayer is much more than that.

We speak to people everyday, yet none of us has ever viewed that as praying to men. Why, then, is it that when we approach angels, we can consider it as praying to them? Jesus commanded us to cast out demons and to instruct demonic strongholds to leave. This is verbal communication. The church does not view this as praying to demons. What, then, is prayer, that sacred, holy intimate communion with our beloved Yeshua?

Prayer should not be confined to just verbal communication. Verbal communication is one avenue of expressing prayer. True prayer is the gaze of the soul upon the face of Jesus Christ. It is the conscious ascension of one's soul into the depths of Yeshua, until one's soul melts into the image of Yeshua. This is prayer; a divine mixture between Creator and creation so that creation can share the bliss of the Creator.

Prayer is the inward gravitating and centering of the soul upon the person of the Lord Jesus Christ. To pray is to abide in Him. We are called to abiding prayer, which is an intimate heart-to-heart exchange with Jesus, which no angel or man is worthy of. It is the practice of the presence of God, the acknowledgement of the person of the Lord Jesus Christ around us, not through words, but through the posture of our hearts. To pray is to raise our hearts toward Him.

YHVH's definition of prayer cannot be attained from the reception of outward voices or repetitive 'Christianese' cliche declarations. We enter into prayer when we inwardly ascend into the depths of Jesus Christ. Based on a deeper and richer understanding of what prayer is, our interaction and communication with angels cannot be defined as praying to them. Therefore, we do not have to be afraid to talk to and interact with angels.

Jesus has made us kings (Revelation 1:6), and as kings, we have the authority to make decrees and declarations. He has assigned the aid of His angels to us, to hearken to the voice of our words. We shall decree a thing and it shall be established.

We are kings and we have a family of angelic beings that are waiting for our interaction. We can talk to them and send them on assignments. Ask the Holy Spirit to reveal them to you. Remember the words of St. Francis de Sale:

"Since God often sends us his inspirations by means of his angels, we ought frequently to offer him our aspirations through the same channel. ... Call on them and honor them frequently, and ask their help in all your affairs, temporal as well as spiritual."

The Lord Jesus Christ is not insecure. He will not be ticked off if we said hello to the angels and begin to get to know them. A true angel of the Lord will always give great honor to the Lord and will carry the frequencies of heaven which are peace, joy, love, holiness, purity, truth, humility, and reverence to the King of kings and the Lord of lords.

There is no fear in love, so fall deeply in love with Jesus, and from that place of intimacy, talk with Him about His angelic canopy. Begin to say hello to the angels and you will begin to see more of the supernatural in your life, guaranteed.

Do I instruct the angels or ask Holy Spirit?

Generally speaking, we have used "prayer" as a default mode to dodge our responsibility to instruct angels. Over the centuries, we have slowly forfeited our responsibilities as sons of God by not working with angels and have thrown everything back to the Lord. A little prayer here and there, and let the heavens move, we have thought apathetically.

The Holy Spirit is our helper (John 14:16). A helper does not do all the work; he is there to assist in response to our effort. If that was not the case, the Lord would not have compelled us to strive to enter His rest, neither would Paul have said that he labored and agonized more than all the apostles (Hebrews 4:11, 1 Corinthians 15:10). There is an agonizing and laboring for all of us, but it is found within the flow of the Holy Spirit. It springs forth from rest.

The beauty in Jesus is that the Spirit has answered our prayers in Christ Jesus, awaiting us to initiate the reality of the answer through His angels. You and I have an innumerable company of angels waiting for our engagement and instructions in and through Christ Jesus.

Moses is a great example of this issue of mankind giving his God-given responsibilities back to the Lord. The Lord rebuked Moses for praying to Him when he (Moses) and Israel stood at the Red Sea with Pharaoh's army behind them (Exodus 15:16). Moses had the staff, which functioned as his scepter of authority over the physical elements of this earth. The Lord often times does not "answer" our prayers because He is waiting for us to take the initiative and understand that we, too, carry Moses' scepter of authority.

"And thou shalt take this rod in thine hand, wherewith thou shalt do signs." *(Exodus 4:17)*

This authority usually comes as the power or right to give orders and instruct high angelic beings. YHVH delegated His authority to Jesus. Jesus has vested all that power and authority upon His lovers, hence the church of Jesus Christ has unfathomable power and authority.

So we are back to the original question: can I instruct the angels or do I ask my Father to do so? Do I have any responsibility as a joint heir with Jesus Christ? Apart from a deeply intimate relationship with precious Holy Spirit, we cannot and should not instruct angels. But in union with Him, we are equipped to do so.

Most of the things we pray for, we are to decree and let angels do the bidding, but angels only run in response to His word.

His Angels Hearken to His Word

**"*Bless the Lord, ye his angels, that excel in strength, that do his commandments, hearkening unto the voice of his word."* (Psalm 103:20-21)

The service or ministry of one's angels is in correspondence to the revelation of God that emanates or flows from the individual. Angels are beings that "hearken to the voice of His word."

The voice of His word is the divinely revealed word of God. The word becomes a voice when it is revealed. It is the revealed word that speaks, not the concealed word, and it is this word that the angels adhere to.

We can only walk in the authority of the Word that is revealed to us. In every revelation of God that we enter into, a crown is given to operate in that revelation. It is this crown that angels respect and honor.

When we walk in a revealed truth from the voice of the word, we have the God-given authority to command angels with our voices. This is because our voices become one with the voice of the Son of God.

Revelation of the Son of God brings us into union with the Word of God. The more we are in divine union with Jesus Christ, the more authority we have to direct angels to *"hearken"* to the voice of His word. Out of oneness and the authority vested upon us by Jesus Christ, we can send angels to task.

Everything flows from oneness with Yeshua, so let our hearts be synchronized with His, and let the beauty of His heartbeat orchestrate our responsibilities of instructing the heavenly hosts of angels at our service.

Prone to worship another, Lord, I fear

"Let no man beguile you of your reward in a voluntary humility and worshipping of angels, intruding into those things which he hath not seen, vainly puffed up by his fleshly mind." (Colossians 2:18)

The heart of man is a huge abyss, which, if not filled with the vision of Jesus, is prone to gravitate to any other power that is supernatural. Due to the record of the fall in us, we are quickly drawn to worship that which is fallen. Whether we want to accept it or not, we were made for more than being mere humans in a physical world who die and then go somewhere.

The fallen nature of man has caused humanity to have a natural propensity to worship something other than YHVH. Worship is one of our default expressions, and this could be seen in the way we idolize or worship a bevy of things. It takes a pure heart to worship Him, because in worship, we behold Him. Beholding Him drains our old Adamic life. God can only be worshipped by those who have residues of His nature, spirit beings born of Him.

"But the hour cometh, and now is, when the true worshippers shall worship the Father in spirit and in truth: for the Father seeketh such to worship him." (John 4:23)

Man, unconsciously and consciously, knows that his identity proceeds from a higher power, thus a deep longing within man's heart is to fully know who he is. Since Adam lost his identity as a son of God, man became infected with that same loss of identity. In the quest to regain it, we see thousands of religious sects that have readily offered an answer to meet the need for worship. All of these originated from fallen angels craving adoration. When I say 'religious,' I also mean satanic or the spirit of the anti-Christ. Religion is anti-Christ.

Any worship, other than that of Yeshua, is rooted in the fall and is the result of a wandering heart searching for purpose and a sense of belonging. Even in our desire to know the angelic canopy, if our hearts are not filled with the vision of Jesus Christ, we are prone to worship angels. Historically, some have given obeisance to fallen angels from which false religions have sprung up. The true, holy angels of the Lord will not accept our worship. Even if we try to do so, they will not accept it.

And I John saw these things, and heard them. And when I had heard and seen, I fell down to worship before the feet of the angel which shewed me these things. Then saith he unto me, See thou do it not: for I am thy fellow servant, and of thy brethren the prophets, and of them which keep the sayings of this book: worship God. (Revelations 22:8-9)

The entire chapter of Colossians 2 is a warning by Paul, particularly in verse 18, that the worship of angels is prohibited. He shows the triumph of the New Covenant that was wrought through Christ. Jesus won the rightful position to have our hearts.

Worship is a lifestyle and a sustained state of giving over our hearts to the Lord. And giving our hearts to any other, including angels, is Luciferian to the core. The enemy has readily prepared a platform for misdirected and misappropriated worship, and it all points to Lucifer.

Worship is also the lifting up of our heart's posture toward Him who sits on the throne; it originates from seeing God and it leads to beholding God. Our hearts need to be fully anchored in Him who is Love. If we do not have a revelation of His worthiness, we may avoid also engaging with the angels for fear of gravitating toward them rather than Yeshua.

The problem is that we have a religious system mechanically wired in our minds about how He deserves to be worshiped. We have been indoctrinated. This, in turn, has led to a mental conception rather than an actual revelation of His worthiness. He is worthy of it all, but to truly walk and live a life in response to His matchless worthiness, one has to see Him. Not just hear about Him, but behold Him. The result of which is an exclamation of awe and wonder graciously transcribed through the posture of one's heart. Let us see the Son who, having received a much better name than the angels, has bestowed upon them who believe on Him, a much better name than the angels.

Chapter 2

Defining Angels:
Heaven's Light Beings

The word 'angel' is the Hebrew 'malach,' which simply means 'messenger.' It is more of a generic name for many beings who operate under the same canopy and have a relatively similar work. These beings exist for the same purpose: to see the will and purposes of YHVH be accomplished. They have been designed to see the smooth running of an eternal household, of things in heaven, things on earth, and things under the earth in all their multitudinous dimensions.

I would define the angelic canopy as a realm of different 'species' of highly advanced and intelligent spiritual beings, crafted from the expressions and attributes of YHVH. It is a heavenly universe that is built upon the principles of a family. It is like a gigantic *family-oriented workforce.* Its branches are vast and too numerous to be comprehended in one lifetime.

The canopy of angels is so great that the majority of them do not fully know each other and some of them have not yet met. Angels continue to grow in stature, character, and functionality. Some are quite playful, with a sense of humor, while others are stern and serious.

They are all spirits, but at the same time, each family of angels has its own particular spiritual substance, specifically designed to manifest the light of Christ. The composition of their spiritual substance differs. Paul shed some light on this when he wrote,

"All flesh is not the same flesh: but there is one kind of flesh of men, another flesh of beasts, another of fishes, and another of birds. There are also celestial bodies, and bodies terrestrial: but the glory of the celestial is one, and the glory of the terrestrial is another." (1 Corinthians 15:39)

All celestial bodies are also not the same. There is one kind of celestial body of men, another celestial body of seraphims, another celestial body of cherubims, and another of zoes, all having their own glory. As species can be classified according to their genetics and body composition, so can angels. They even differ in the makeup of their spirits. There are also different races of angels, imbued with different languages, depending on their varying assignments and mandates. There is one language for seraphim, another for cherubim, and so on. Let me explain.

Since heaven is a higher dimension than this earthly plain, it has a higher form of communication and higher intelligence. Since angels are beings made from the creative light of the living Christ, they are lights personified; therefore, their thinking and processing faculties are faster than that of mankind. Hence, there is a need for languages which speak and convey depths of comprehension at that same heavenly frequency at which they process information.

The dimension of the heavens will not bend to my earthly Adamic form of communication, I have to yield to heaven's ways. Heaven has specific ways of communication. Let us take a look at tongues.

Tongues and Angels

"Though I speak with the tongues of men and of angels..." (1 Corinthians 13:1)

There are tongues specifically formulated for us by the Holy Spirit to aid us in interacting with angels. These are tongues of angels, the means by which certain families of angels interact with one another and with us.

In heaven, instructions are not given as they are in our earthly lives, but rather, they are imparted. When God instructs angels or us to do something, within that *word of instruction* is the energy and graces for the instruction to play forth its purpose. The instruction is not independently achieved and fulfilled through the sheer brilliance or power of the angels; rather, it becomes an external personification of YHVH's word within the angels' spiritual makeup. Nothing can be done apart from His Word, and let us also remember that a word is merely a *thought expressed.* Tongues of angels administered by sons of YHVH are divine thoughts expressed that find a personification within angels' spiritual makeups.

In the spiritual worlds, thoughts speak and convey sounds, but the impact and effect of each expressed thought is different. Certain spirits have not yet reached a maturity level to absorb, listen to, and comprehend the high energy thoughts of other spirit beings, so there is a need to vocally express the thoughts. On the other hand, for high energy angels to fully comprehend our thoughts, they need to flow forth from us at higher heavenly frequencies. YHVH has given us the gift of tongues in order for us to release our thoughts at heavenly frequencies.

The scripture says that we do not know how to pray as we ought to, but the Spirit intercedes for us with wordless groaning (Romans 8:26). *Tongues* are the sheathing of our physical tongues by the power of the Holy Spirit, to allow deeper and quicker forms of conveying the intent of a message. There is a place where prayer goes deeper than mere words, and this is where the element of sound comes in. This bypasses our natural mind and the need to formulate words to express intent and depth. The core for speaking in tongues is not really the words, but the frequency of the intent, translated as another language. I have found that the gift of tongues is fundamental in aiding us to instruct and engage with angels accordingly.

Tongues, rather than being a method, have to do with conveying meaning, complex ideas, and the true essence of a message. Tongues of angels are various languages of different species of angels that best express and illustrate different aspects of revelations, truths, and thoughts. They create an efficient, fast, and understandable way of interacting with the Kingdom of light and its holy beings.

Just as every earthly family has specific gestures and ways of communication that are unique to them, so it is with angelic families. In every family of the angelic order, there are various tongues used to address and engage in that realm. To bring clarity to the use and importance of engaging with angels in tongues, let me share one of my favorite experiences.

It was sometime in 2016 when I was deep in worship for a couple of hours. I asked the Lord to give me tongues to speak to the family of angels who bear the name 'Found One,' as I had literally met this angel, or an angel from this family. To my amazement, I immediately found myself speaking and calling several different names. By intuition, I knew they were names of angels and the place was filled with several angels. My eyes were open into that realm, and I saw some really interesting things.

There was an angel standing by the doorway, and as my mother entered the room, she walked right through him. The angel put on a funny, startled look and smiled as if to say, "Why didn't she acknowledge my presence?" His expression, though, had no connotations of condemnation, but rather seemed to literally exude joy to the point where my mom and I burst into laughter. Then I saw an angel who seemed to bear a strong resemblance to lightning, like he was handcrafted by lightning. His skin seemed to have the intense of white light or hues from lightning. It seemed as if lightning had been captured within his body; most likely, he was an angel who energizes and brings swift, lightning-effect responses.

I asked the Holy Spirit to show me how to instruct him and I began to speak in new tongues. What I saw was something amazing. The tongues that I was saying through the Holy Spirit seemed to ride upon the *sound waves* of my voice and went right into him. His very being became a receptacle for my words. I began to see that my words became the fuel of locomotion in the angel's body in relation to his next assignment. Their vibration seemed to be energy that fused itself into the very makeup of the angel's being. He did not seem to receive the words as we would with our ears. The sound of the words seemed to literally enter into and become part of him.

I began to understand that the words I had spoken to him became part of his genetic makeup and would influence the way he flowed. It brought much clarity to how angels receive instructions. Further clarification showed me that his spiritual makeup was not meant to receive *any other tongues*. There were grooves, channels, or veins that were built within his being, and as as I released these specific tongues, the energy of my words would become embedded within these grooves. He and the tongues seem to become one so that his actions and movements were synchronized to the words that I had spoken and the words became his "blood" or "his energy flow." The veins of his spiritual makeup were so designed and molded to only receive these *specific angelic tongues*.

I have also come to understand that sometimes when we pray in tongues, we are literally reading the contents of our destiny scroll to our angels. After all, it was Jesus Christ, the Living Word Himself, who wrote or encoded our destiny scroll within our spirit man. The continuous expanding of our spirit man is the breaking forth of our destiny scroll. There are scroll watcher angels who have been assigned and are committed to aiding us in fulfilling our scrolls.

Read out your spirit man to your angel in tongues today; read out those 'nitty gritty' truths of His person He has lavishly written all over your spirit!

Reminiscing

I remember when I met my angel for the first time. I cannot recall ever consciously meeting him before, but the moment I looked at him, I knew who he was. Found One's persona was very stern, with an air of, "I am here to fulfill my mandate." It seemed as if he was not there to joke around, even though, later on, he cordially smiled in response to a request I had made. There was a strong aura of deep, reverential fear of the Lord that exuded from him. This made me approach him cautiously.

In the few moments I was with him, I was careful about how to address him. I was in awe, wondering how it was that he had been with me all this time, and yet now, in this vision, I was even afraid to address him. The key to truly honoring the angels is to develop a relationship with them and not to take them for granted. Even though we can develop friendship with them, we must be careful to approach them with respect and honor, which is a path of true sonship.

We must also be cognizant that we cannot go about commanding the angels at our whim and fancy. That is a sure sign of immaturity. We need to be illuminated by the light of Christ to be aware of, interact with, and embrace the mysteries of the Kingdom of YHVH.

The scriptures say that the angel of the Lord encamps round about those who fear Him. When we begin to embrace the truth of the encampment of angels around us, there will be a heightened awareness which will increase and enhance our interaction with them.

One night, in my kitchen, I turned my consciousness into the spirit realm. I saw four angels and slowly began to communicate with them. One angel, who was standing by the stove, seemed to be journaling. I looked at him and asked what he was writing. "You!" came the playful response. "What about me?" I asked, "Your life," he said, "a record for the King (Jesus). Don't you know that every minute and second of your life He treasures and holds them intimately within Himself? There are no wasted years in Jesus."

I gently walked toward the angel, with arms wide open intending to hug him. About two feet from him, I realized he had a certain canopy around him, which seemed to be the aura of heaven he carried, made from joy. I burst into laughter, as effortlessly I became enveloped into this canopy and streams of joy cascaded through me.

I realized that joy is also a sign of angelic manifestation in a place. There are moments when I see or sense my angels, and it seems as if they carry a strong energy of pure joy which eventually floods my being.

Joy is a fruit of the Spirit, and the fruits of the Spirit are also the manifestation of heaven's atmosphere. Oftentimes, the angels that I have met have carried a certain aura of a fruit of the Spirit. Hence, everything that flows from the spiritual world of Yeshua carries within itself measures of the impartations of the fruits.

Whenever you find yourself experiencing an outward expression of a fruit of the Spirit around you, most likely, it is an angel who is ministering to you. Sometimes in prayer and worship, we may see flashes of light darting across the room; I often see these in my peripheral vision. These are angels ascending and descending faster than the speed of light in response to our prayer.

How many of us have felt a wind blow into a room during times of worship? I certainly have. It is an angel who is ministering to you, for after all,

"He makes his Angels the wind and his ministers burning fire." (Psalm 104:4, Aramaic Version)

I have had moments where I have walked into church services and seen gigantic balls of fire; more like miniature suns or circular lights. Many persons have experienced these and called them "orbs of light." The angel that William Branham* encountered first appeared as a small ball of fire, and from within it, a man of about 200 pounds stepped out.*

There are always angels on assignment around us. They are innumerable, with varying classifications, purposes, and mandates. We are privileged to interact with these celestial beings within the Kingdom of YHVH, so let us not fear to step into our supernatural inheritance.

The Difference Between Sons and Angels

Have you ever wondered what is the difference between men and angels? Is it because they are spirits? Are we not spirit beings, as well? Maybe it's because they have wings? According to the Psalmist, YHVH has wings.

"He shall cover thee with his feathers, and under his wings shalt thou trust: his truth shall be thy shield and buckler." (Psalms 91:4).

I certainly don't. Do you? If God has wings, and angels have wings, who then looks more like God? Us or them? I have also heard people say, "It's because we have the Holy Spirit in us and angels don't." Is that really true? Was not Lucifer an anointed cherub? And is not the anointing the essence of the person of the Holy Spirit? Angels to a certain degree have the Holy Spirit. Angelic acts are infused by the Holy Spirit. So what differentiates us from angels?

The difference is that we are sons. Simply put, we are God's kids, but we are sons who willingly serve because of love. Angels are servants of a high order, but being servants is not at all a derogatory position; it is a position of humility. Jesus Christ Himself exemplifies this as Servant King.

A servant is in a household to serve in the position for which he is hired. Thus, a servant works in a particular area of the household. His influence is limited within that position he exists for. Angels work more or less like this. These beings are fully formulated to stand and function in the names they carry, never violating or breaking their ranks. Sometimes they are there for a very specific task. They will not deviate from that assignment. Their functionality is contained within their assignment. This is why sometimes an angel may see one going through spiritual attacks and not do anything about it, if it's not his mandate. Sons, on the other hand, have free access to all areas of the house.

It was my angel Found One who cordially said to me, "Angels are made in an attribute and aspect of God's image and mankind is made in the image of God. When the scriptures say that you are made in the image of God, it doesn't mean that you already look like God. But rather it means that the spirit of man is the only spirit that has the capacity to fully embrace and carry the full spectrums of the light of Christ. One of Adam's mandates was to fully grow into the full spectrum of the glory of YHVH. *(The actual Hebrew meaning of the words 'image and likeness' in Genesis 1:26-28 mean to be conformed to a likeness. Thus Adam was to have a perpetual growth into the full stature of YHVH.)*

"Angels are beings who are created in a particular aspect of the image of God. For example, the angel of goodness is molded in and from a higher degree of YHVH's goodness. He can only bring that particular spectrum of Christ's light that he was created in. The angel Goodness can only be goodness and cannot carry the light spectrums of the angel Recorder, or Winds of Change. Men's spirits, on the other hand, have the capacity to fully embrace and carry all the light spectrums of YHVH, for example, goodness, recorder, breakthrough, winds of change, etc. Other angels grow into that aspect of YHVH that they were created to stand and operate in."

The intricate design of our spirit man is that it can be fully flooded with the Light of Yeshua to the capacity that the intensities, frequencies, and spectrums of Yeshua's light can dwell fully within us. God dwells in unapproachable light (1 Timothy 6:16); thus, the structure of God's house is light. But not just any light;

unapproachable light! Jesus is this light (John 1:7; 8:12) which we are commanded to walk in and be clothed with.

"But if we walk IN the light as He is IN the light, we have fellowship with one another, and the blood of Jesus His Son cleanses us from all sin." (1 John 1:7)

This is what it means to be the house of YHVH: to allow Jesus, the unapproachable Light, to flood our entire being.

Being flooded with the Light of Christ means that we will vibrate at the frequency of the unapproachable light in which YHVH dwells, hence, we have the capacity to approach and fellowship with Him, as we in turn become "unapproachable" light beings. Men's spirit, being in the image of God, has the divine graces to fully vibrate at divine frequencies in higher degrees than the angels.

Angels radiate the light of an attribute and nature of Yeshua from which they are made. Since man's spirit is made in and from all the inexhaustible and immeasurable attributes of YHVH, we have the capacity to fully radiate the glories of the Light of all God's attributes.

Jesus is the fullness of YHVH; hence, within the person of the Lord Jesus Christ are all the inexhaustible attributes of God. The culmination of these immeasurable attributes of YHVH have an image and it is the face of Jesus Christ. As He is, so are we (1 John 4:7). One of the ways Yeshua manifested His attributes was through creating celestial beings who mirror these attributes. Angels shine forth the attribute and image of YHVH that they are made in, while we can shine forth His *entire* image and attributes. This is the difference between the spirit of men and that of angels.

The story is told of Daniel's meeting with an angel by the river, and the intensities of the glories that the angel carried caused Daniel to drop as one dead (Daniel 8:17). This angel came to Daniel in an aspect of the image of YHVH from which the angel was created and formulated.

What, then, shall we look like if we allow our spirit man to be fully immersed and flooded with the light of the image of YHVH?

God's attributes are unparalleled and infinite; thus, there is no limit to the number of angels formulated to stand and operate in these attributes. The angelic canopy is ever expanding, as our Father is constantly revealing new attributes of His nature and person. There is no manifestation of an attribute of God that is not accompanied by an order of angels who stand within that attribute.

God is good, so there is an angel who is assigned to the realm of the goodness of Yahweh; his function is an extension of the hand of YHVH's goodness. This angel is made to reflect the image of YHVH's goodness. God is glorious, so there is an angel who is assigned to the realms of the glory of Yahweh. God is merciful, so there is an angel who is assigned to the realm of Yahweh's mercy. Our God's attributes are inexhaustible and infinite; hence, the canopy of angels awaiting the believer is innumerable.

"Of the increase of his government and peace there shall be no end." (Isaiah 9: 7)

Knowing the Role and Function of Angels

"Neither can they die any more: for they are equal unto the angels; and are children of God, being children of the resurrection." (Luke 20:36)

"But I know that my lord the king is like an angel of God, so do what you think is best." (2 Samuel 19:27, NLT)

"But my lord has wisdom like the wisdom of the angel of God to know all things that are on the earth." (2 Samuel 14:20, ESV)

"And all that sat in the council, looking steadfastly on him, saw his face as it had been the face of an angel." (Acts 6:15)

In terms of the inheritance that we have received in Jesus as sons, we have been made greater than the angels, but in terms of functionality and sheer intelligence, they surpass us. There is a particular aspect and functionality of angels that mankind has to enter into while in this earthly metacosm.

Our godly character, which I call the nature of Jesus Christ, is as a result of the impartations of the life of Christ through the person of the Holy Spirit. It is molded and worked out through trials and obedience. However, there is a supernatural dimension of how angels operate that my spirit man has to tap into. The reason why we have been largely unable to operate in the capacity of the angels is because of the death process that entered mankind through Adam. We are spirit beings, whom outside of Jesus, are all dying.

Jesus said,

"In the resurrection we will not die but are equal to the angels." (Luke 20:36)

Jesus is not merely talking about the cancellation of death being the basis of our equality with angels. Yeshua is talking about all the depraved residues of death that keep us from fully functioning as new creation beings. The equality is in terms of operation and function.

The resurrection is not a day, a date, nor a future event, but a Person (John 11:25), in whom we put on immortality and become equal in operation and functionality with the angels. When we enter into Resurrection personified, Christ Jesus, the death process is cancelled. The reason that death's residue seems to remain in us is because we still bear the consciousness of the first Adam. This awareness of the fall has been passed into our souls. The curse of death cannot reside in the same space as resurrection life. Therefore, the absence of death in YHVH's angels' spiritual makeup allows them to operate in a more powerful capacity than us.

Our chief guardian angel is there to reveal the capacity of the vastness and operation of our spirit man through his actions, and in doing so, he aids in the tutoring of our spirit man to enter into what YHVH has called us to do in a particular season of our life.

For instance, if we have an angel who brings laughter, his spiritual makeup is literally crafted as the laughter of YHVH, and this shows that God is bringing seasons of laughter into our life. It is *not only* allowing the ministry of the angel, but it is also allowing a part of his essence to merge into our spirit man. It is not the spirit of the angel that our spirit man has to merge into, but it is his specific operation and workings. Hence, we can grow into the functionality and flow of the angel Laughter.

The Holy Spirit is constantly bringing our spirit man into perpetual growth so that we can vibrate the various light spectrums that the angels carry. One of the ways to fully understand this is by knowing how the ministry of impartation works. There are different channels of impartation, but I want to give a glimpse into angelic impartation.

When a person lays hands upon us, they are releasing a measure of the gift in which they operate. The angel that aids them in the operation of the gift ministers that facet of the light of Christ which that angel carries. Remember, the light that the angels carry denotes their form and function.

For example, take the gift of revelation. If someone is receiving revelation from YHVH, it is because an angel who carries that light spectrum from YHVH has become an instrument of impartation for that person. This enables one to enter into the angel's domain of operation.

When that individual prays for you, the angel will impart a measure of the light of that component of his service, thus enabling your spirit man to enter into it. This, in turn, causes your spirit man to radiate at the frequencies of that light of revelation. An angel from the same family of revelation is now assigned to you, drawn by the frequencies of the light of revelation emanating from you. Every gift imparted carries frequencies of light that draw the angels.

For further clarity, an angel called Breakthrough is not only in your life to bring breakthrough. He stands as a testimony and a witness that your spirit man has the full-fledged capacity to operate like he does by entering the realm of breakthrough. Your spirit man is thus enabled to merge into the realm of the angel and become equal to him.

When angels came to minister to Jesus in the wilderness, as the Son of man, it was more like a divine transfer of a particular function of the angels (Mark 1:13). In the garden, before our Lord's great trial, an angel came to strengthen Him. I believe, without a shadow of a doubt, that the angel was formed and crafted in the strength of YHVH; hence, the angel transferred into Jesus' soul an aspect of his (the angel's) functionality which was the strength of YHVH, administered as deep abiding joy.

God's desire is that our spirit man should develop into the aspect of the operation of the angels ministering to us. For this to happen, the angel has to reveal his nature to you, mostly through the service he performs. I have an angel called Found One, but over time, I have come to understand that Found One is not necessarily his name, but the name of the service he brings to me. He is an angel who finds and restores lost files, mysteries, and documents that the church lost over the ages. This is one of my mandates as a son of God, to be a custodian of heavenly files.

We can know what YHVH is releasing to us, or what he has called us to be in a particular season, by the angel He has assigned. The endless discoveries of the depths of the Son allows us to meet different angels that are to impart and bring a revelation of what they carry. And the gift of discernment is crucial for this.

Discernment of spirits is more than differentiating the good from the evil spirits; it is a gift that allows us to fully comprehend and know the angels that are in a particular place. We can also discern the purpose or the mandate of an angel by how he may be configured. I met an angel called Winds of Change; his spiritual makeup was literally crafted as the winds of YHVH. *Electric-light-energy-winds* formed his being! And when he spoke, his voice was like visible electric winds!

The Name of an Angel

Every miracle and supernatural demonstration of Jesus is a glimpse of a life of interacting with angels. Let us look further into how the function of an angel is linked to its name. A name always speaks of the character and nature of something. It was Michael who fought the devil, not Raphael, Gabriel, Uriel, or any of the glorious cherubim. This is not because Michael is the most powerful angel, but it was because of his office and calling. His office was and is his name, and his name means 'Who is like God?'

Keep in mind, the crime of Lucifer was trying to be like God instead of honouring and embracing the purpose for which God created him. (Isaiah 14:14). Michael stood and functioned in the office which brought great reverence to the Creator by operating and showing to all angels that nothing is and no being can be like God, apart from God. Here stood a high ranking cherubim with a desire to be like God, to co-exist and co-rule with God — a position which no angel was ever created for. The angel who functioned in the office of "who is like God?" fought the enemy, denouncing that it was not possible for this cherub to be like God.

If the devil's crime was to try to recreate or manipulate matter and energy outside the will of YHVH, an angel who functions in the role of matter and energy would have withstood Satan. Angels' mandates, influence, and purposes are confined within the names they carry.

An angel's name is not just the name of a single angel, but also a collective name of a group of angels who exist to carry the same mandate. It is more of a family name.

In every group of angels, there is a "parent" angel, and the angels under him carry his name. A parent angel oversees other angels who are under him. His authority and purpose is so great that he is able to impart measures of his spirit to the angels that he is in charge of. The majority who are under him work as "surrogates." Thus, they deputize for the head or parent angel in a specific role or office, by carrying his mandate through the impartations of his spirit and name, thereby also delegating to them his God-given authority.

For instance, the scriptures talk about Michael and his angels. Michael is the head or parent angel to a group of angels who stand for warfare purposes. The angels that are under Michael also carry his name, and in this, they carry his nature, character, and form of operation.

Someone in one part of the world might encounter "Michael," and yet his description of Michael differs from another person's, simply because they have both encountered the *surrogate* versions of Michael. We see the same heavenly pattern when God named the 12 tribes of Israel. Individuals were identified by the names of the tribes to which they belonged. For instance, the tribe of Judah consisted of direct descendants of Judah. Judah was their parent. This is the same pattern when it comes to angelic families: the parent angel, being the one from which the family bears its name, and the angels under him, being his surrogates. These angelic surrogates are able to host measures of the spirit of their parent angel.

The relationship and connection between the cherubim and the wheels within wheels in Ezekiel can help us in understanding the role of head angels and surrogate angels. Let's look at Ezekiel 1:20:

"Wherever the spirit was to go, they went, there was their spirit to go; and the wheels were lifted up with them: for the spirit of the living creatures was in the wheels."

Do you notice something? The spirit of the cherubim and not the Holy Spirit was in the wheels. The wheels themselves are living beings, which are also called the "ophanim." I believe the ophanim are surrogates to the cherubim as they are receptors and carriers of the cherubim spirit.

An angelic surrogate is an angel who is specifically there to carry a measure of his head/parent angel's spirit and deputize for him. You also have surrogates, and they look like you!

Chapter 3

The Files of Angels

"*And the servant of God looked on the angel of God, and, conversing with him face to face familiarly, even as with a friend, asked who he was, and by what name was he called. And the heavenly messenger answered that he was the ministering spirit of the Lord, sent into the world to minister unto them who have the heritage of salvation; that he was called Victor, and especially deputed to the care of him, and he promised to be his helpmate and his assistant in doing all things. And although it is not needful that heavenly spirits should be called by human names, yet the angel, being beautifully clothed with a human form composed of the air, called himself Victor, for that he had received from Christ, the most victorious King, the power of vanquishing and binding the powers of the air and the princes of darkness; who had also given to his servants made of the potter's clay the power of treading on serpents and scorpions, and of vanquishing and bruising Satan.*" (The Life and the Acts of Saint Patrick: The Archbishop, Primate, and Apostle of Ireland)

"*From the first, in all parts and in all forms, God spoke with our fathers by The Prophets, And in these last days he has spoken with us by his Son, whom he ordained The Heir of all things, and by him he made the universe. For he is The Brilliance of his glory, The Image of his Being, and upholds all things by the power of his word; and he in his Essential Being has accomplished the purification of our sins, and he sat down at the right hand of the Majesty on high. * And This One is altogether greater than the Angels, according to how much more excellent than theirs is The Name which he possesses.*"

For to which one of the Angels did God ever say, 'You are my Son; today I have begotten you', and again, 'I shall be to him The Father and he shall be to me the Son'?

Again, when he brings The Firstborn into the universe, he says, 'All the Angels of God shall worship him.'

But he spoke in this way about the Angels: 'He makes his Angels the wind and his Ministers the burning fire.'

But concerning The Son, he said, 'Your throne, oh God, is to the eternity of eternities. A straight scepter is the scepter of your Kingdom.'

You have loved righteousness and you have hated evil; because of this, God, your God, has anointed you with the oil of a joy beyond your companions.

And again, 'You have laid the foundation of The Earth from the beginning and the Heavens are the work of your hands.'

Those shall pass away and you remain, and they all shall wear out like a robe,

And you shall fold them up like a cloak; they shall be changed, and you are as you are*; your years shall not end.

But to which of the Angels did he ever say, 'Sit at my right hand until I put your enemies as a footstool under your feet'?

Behold, are they not all spirits of service, who are sent into service for the sake of those who are going to inherit life?" (St. Paul)

There are countless angelic libraries in heaven which are like entire cities of networked angelic schools. When I first set out to write this book, my initial desire was to bring to the surface some of the mysteries contained within the volumes of the books of the angels in heaven.

If we were to find ourselves within reach of the shelves of the angelic libraries, there would be book upon book, scroll upon scroll of different angelic stories. I am certain that we would see books on The History and the Mysteries of Earth, The Creation of Angels, The Fall of Lucifer, The Origin of Darkness, the Beauty of the Cross, Understanding Mankind, and so on. These are what I have come to call "Angelic Files," countless scrolls that allow angels to have insight and understanding into mankind's position in the multi-verses.

The cross of Jesus Christ was the greatest elevation of mankind, and to date, this elevation still awes the angels. I believe that since Jesus, through the cross, has made us *"fellow citizens with the saints, and of the household of God" (Ephesians 2:19),* it is our sole responsibility to understand the environment of our original abode. This is the environment that was solely designed for us. This is the spiritual world of Yeshua.

This spiritual universe of Yeshua is not an empty abyss. It contains a well-choreographed network of different species and races of angelic beings. Whether we want to accept it or not, being fully immersed in the spiritual universes of Yeshua means that we will consciously, unconsciously, or subconsciously interact with angels, and be found reading some of their materials. I would rather interact with angels and look into the angelic libraries consciously.

I remember one day when the Lord granted me the opportunity to teach a class of young, maturing angels. I deputized for the lead angel, who stood next to me for the entire duration. It was awesome and epic! There was an air of excitement and the tangible presence of the Lord was in the atmosphere. Their reception of me was like no other I have ever experienced before. The innocent passion and desire in this group of youthful 'student angels' of wanting to know about Him was stupendous. They carried a strong culture of honor. I taught them a little about what I know about the Blood of Jesus.

I believe there is nothing as fascinating to angels as when a son of YHVH takes the initiative of searching out the mysteries of our God. In doing so, we are unconsciously also revealing these mysteries to various angels around us — after all, Saint Peter said of them,

"which things the angels desire to look into." (1 Peter 1:12)

In perceiving and learning from any branch of the angelic libraries of heaven, we are simply to mature and grow from the continuous expression of the Living Word. And all that the angels eagerly desire to look into is the mysteries contained in the Living Word, unveiled and perfectly wrapped within a son of God. They, too, desire to be close to Him and know Him. He is the fascination of all creation.

Now, the Word Himself is truth and the Word Himself is the Light of understanding. Let us sit together once more, allowing the weight of His beauty to animate the scriptures, making us consciously perceive and understand the *Angelic Files* from His voice within the scriptures.

Chapter 4

The First Sphere of the Family of Angels

When God gave His Son (John 3:16), He gave the literal Living Life of Himself to the world, and He also gave the endless expressions of service from the attributes of the Son, personified in and by angelic beings.

The angelic canopy has been given to mankind to aid and assist us, saved or unsaved. But there are certain angels who solely minister to the redeemed. There are also certain angels whose ministry is for those who have consciously plunged into the depths of the Son.

The truth is that we are born again in Heavenly places, but we do not begin our journeys within the depths of the Son. The pursuit of the depths of His heart, where the mysteries of YHVH are contained, is initiated by desire. *To the degree that you desire something intimately in your heart, you can enter into its reality.* We have to desire to know Life Himself, to plunge ourselves into the essence of His being.

Within His depths is the blazing refining fires which mold and bring forth mature sons, full-fledged brothers of Jesus Christ. This journey of sonship will take us from the crown of thorns to the golden crown of Jesus, from the ash heap to a King's throne (1 Samuel 2:8), from earth's metacosm to YHVH's throne room.

His throne room is a magnificent place, pulsating with Life Himself in His majesty; fearsome, dreadful, yet majestic beings are seen ministering to YHVH. If we are going to rule and reign with Him, it is important that we get to know these fearsome angels around His throne. I believe these same angels will surround our thrones as we co-rule and co-reign with Jesus. These high-energy angelic beings in the throne room comprise the first sphere of angels, and they are custodians of His throne. These are angels who have a first hand revelation of God, administered by YHVH Himself.

We know that the seraphim worship from *above* His throne (Isaiah 6:2).The cherubim are *carriers* of the throne; the King is seated above them (Ezekiel 1:26). The four living creatures or zoes *surround* the throne (Revelation 4:6) and the angels of His presence are *before* His throne (Revelation 8:2). Four uniquely similar but different angels surround His throne: above, below, around, and before.

The Seraphim

"... Beside me, on the left hand, appeared an angel in bodily form... He was not tall but short, and very beautiful; and his face was so aflame that he appeared to be one of the highest rank of angels, who seem to be all on fire... In his hands I saw a great golden spear, and at the iron tip there appeared to be a point of fire. This he plunged into my heart several times... and left me utterly consumed by the great love of God. The pain was so severe that it made me utter several moans. The sweetness caused by this intense pain is so extreme that one cannot possibly wish it to cease, nor is one's soul then content with anything but God. This is not a physical, but a spiritual pain, though the body has some share in it - even a considerable share..." (Theresa of Avila)

"Above him were seraphim, each with six wings: With two wings they covered their faces, with two they covered their feet, and with two they were flying." (Isaiah 6:2)

Jesus promised a baptism of fire to His beloved, which I believe to be a different yet deeper baptism of the Holy Spirit. The baptism of His fire is the baptism of the fire of His love, reserved for those who have allowed Him to find His lover in them. This baptism of fire involves the ministry of the seraphim.

As much as the baptism of fire carry signs and wonders, its greatest and most potent manifestation is the passionate and burning love of God that is imprinted within our hearts when the seraphim touch us. This burning, passionate, vehemently violent love of God will burn within and without until we are pillars of burning, passionate love for Him and all creation.

The root meaning of seraphim is "fiery love," hence the seraphim are fiery beings, clothed within the blazing, bright flames of YHVH. They are aflame with purity, holiness, and love. Since they are above His throne, they behold Him who dwells in unapproachable light with a greater intensity, to the extent that they themselves have literally become beings of the fire of His love. They have a ministry of divine love and holiness which marks hearts blazing hot, and which are consumed with the fire of the love of God. This love is one that separates, setting them apart and fully consecrated to God in pure holiness.

Their worship to YHVH is an unceasing spontaneous response to the purity of His love and holiness that they mirror and burn from. The intensity of the purity of God in them releases the purest and most sublime worship. These beings, like blazing torches, closely resemble the seven spirits of YHVH burning before Him. The seraphim burn above and the spirits burn before. The fire that has given them their spiritual makeup is the fire of His holiness, which is the same fire from which the seven lamps burn (Revelation 4:5). God is the holiest, and a blazing fire that consumes all that is not holy.

To embrace the ministry of the seraphim is to be tutored in holiness, branded and perfected in love as a blazing flame. John the Baptist (John 5:35) and Isaiah (Isaiah 6:7) embraced their ministry. The disciples, waiting in the upper room, were marked by tongues of fire from the seraphim; they violently burned for YHVH and terraformed their worlds (Acts 2:3).

Jesus, on the day of Pentecost, introduced the full-blown ministry of the seraphim into His church. And on that same day, Peter quoted Joel 2:30:

"And I will show wonders in the heavens and in the earth, blood, and fire and pillars of smoke."

As the wonders mentioned by Joel may denote catastrophic signs, I believe that they also speak of the signs and wonders of the ministry of the seraphim. In Isaiah's vision (Isaiah 6:4), when the seraphim (the burning ones) worshipped, the pillars of the temple trembled and smoke filled the temple at the sound of their voices. Some of the signs of the seraphim among us are fire and smoke, glory clouds, coals of fire, and fiery feathers, bringing forth a generation of "souled" out radical lovers of Yeshua who have encountered the burning ones and have been baptized in the fire of His consuming love.

The seraphim have come. And like John the Baptist, the Apostles, and Isaiah, I too embrace the ministry of the seraphim.

"Lord, I embrace and allow the ministry of the seraphim. Let my heart be set ablaze for You, Jesus, in holiness and purity. Burn me away with Your love, YHVH, as I willingly make myself vulnerable to the ministry of the seraphim. Lord, I want to be a torch. As You said of John, 'He was a burning and shining light.' I too want to be Your burning and shining light, Jesus!"

The Cherubim

When we speak of the cherubim, we speak of God's glory. These beings are carriers of the glory of God, and seats of rest for the sons of God. They each have four faces and four wings, and they are covered with eyes. They are like four angels fused together as one. Their ministry belongs to those who minister intimately to YHVH before the Ark of His Presence in heaven.

These four-faced angels transcend the three-dimensional spectrum, energizing the sons who are seated upon them. We, as God's children, are supposed to flow from within the nature of the cherubim.The energies and glories they impart to us enable us to transcend the three-dimensional properties of this cosmos (Ezekiel 1:26). If we dwell and minister to YHVH within the heavenly Ark (Revelation 11:19), we will possess a cherubic nature.

The cherubim were the ones placed at the entrance of the garden along with the flaming swords that turned *"every which way"* in order to guard the way of the Tree of Life.

When we come to Jesus, we do not automatically partake of the Tree of Life. If that was the case, the Lord would not have said to us in Revelation 2:7,

"He that hath an ear, let him hear what the Spirit saith unto the churches; To him that overcometh will I give to eat of the tree of life, which is in the midst of the paradise of God."

Partaking of the Tree of Life is as a result of a life lived within the shadows and the covering of the cherubim. This is a life of overcoming and going through the flaming sword -- a sword that turns every which way -- *judging* everything within us. It is a sword that bars and slays the *"Adam"* within us, and by Adam, I mean self. Adam is not allowed to enter into the garden, because in his fallen state, he cannot partake of the Tree of Life. The sword is there to prevent and to kill Adam. It is a sword that overcomes, conquers, and kills him. The first man that needs to be conquered is the Adam in us.

Only fire can go through fire, hence only "man aflame" can go through the flaming sword which changes our nature. Going through the flaming sword is being allowed to walk "the way of the Tree of Life." This is a life of deep Christian mysticism, for the way of the Tree of Life incorporates in itself the engagement and the interaction with the four living creatures. These creatures are full of eyes, eyes that are doorways into the experiential knowledge of Jesus Christ. The way of the Tree of Life is a way of the mystic secrets of God, administered and revealed by Holy Spirit through the ministry of the four living creatures. Jesus Christ is the mystic secret of God (Colossians 2:3).

The Four Living Creatures

"And before the throne there was a sea of glass like unto crystal: and in the midst of the throne, and round about the throne, were four beasts full of eyes before and behind. And the first beast was like a lion, and the second beast like a calf, and the third beast had a face as a man, and the fourth beast was like a flying eagle." (Revelations 4:6-7)

Of all the majestic and powerful beings around the throne of YHVH, these four distinct beings, with six wings and features that closely resemble the cherubim, have fascinated me most. Their appearance is rather terrifying yet, intriguing. What has totally captivated me is their inclusion in singing the song of the redeemed.

"And when he had taken the book, the four beasts and twenty four elders fell down before the Lamb, having every one of them harps, and golden vials full of

odours, which are the prayers of the saints. And they sung a new song saying, Thou art worthy to take the book, and to open the seals thereof; for thou wast slain, and hast redeemed us to God by thy blood out of every kindred, and tongue, and people, and nation." (Revelation 5:9)

God made a covenant with Noah and all of creation, which was an establishment of the manifestation of His redemptive attributes to all animate creation. He redeemed all things to Himself in His Son. This pattern of heaven has to be mirrored on earth; in heaven, there is a remnant of the redeemed animate creation. This remnant is rather different, as it is more a representation or culmination of all the redeemed four divisions of animate creation, personified in these high angelic beings.

The Lord said to Noah,

"Now behold, I Myself do establish My covenant with you, and with your descendants after you and with every living creature that is with you, the birds, the cattle, and every beast of the earth with you; of all that comes out of the ark, even every beast of the earth'… God said, 'This is the sign of the covenant which I am making between Me and you and every living creature that is with you, for all successive generations; I set My rainbow in the cloud, and it shall be for a sign of a covenant between Me and the earth.'" (Genesis 9:9-10, 11)

YHVH clearly mentions the four main divisions of animate creation here: the birds, the cattle, the beasts, and the man represented by Noah. And then he sets a rainbow as a reminder to creation of his covenant with us. Remember, there is a rainbow around His throne.

The chief of the beasts is the lion, the chief of all the cattle is the ox, and the chief of the birds is the eagle. Then we have God's crowned creation, man. The four living creatures have a face like a man, a lion, an ox, and an eagle. Unlike the cherubim, which has a fusion of four faces, they each have one face.

Each living creature before YHVH's throne is distinct in its character and personality, and each represents a remnant of the four divisions of creation. They are a representative of the full expression of a redeemed remnant of creation.

The four living creatures are partakers of the covenant of Christ. These four beasts are a full culmination of all created living creatures. They stand before the throne of YHVH as a reminder that He has set a covenant in which He has redeemed all things to Himself by the blood of His Son.

"And having made peace through the blood of His cross, by Him to reconcile all things unto Himself; by Him, whether they be things in earth, or things in heaven..." (Colossians 1:20)

The bodies of the four living creatures are covered with eyes, and these eyes are those that have looked and seen into the knowledge of God. In this manner, and since they represent a remnant of the four main divisions of animate creation, they *are partly* a fulfilment of Habakkuk 2:14:

"For the earth shall be filled with the knowledge of the glory of the LORD, as the waters cover the sea."

Engaging within one of their eyes is to look into deep oceans of endless knowledge of the glories of YHVH. They are a full expression of the knowledge of God.

The four living creatures' eyes within (Revelation 4:6) are eyes that search into the depths of YHVH. They are an angelic manifestation of the seeking nature of the Holy Spirit. *"The Spirit searches into everything, even the depths of God"* (1 Corinthians 2:10). The Person of the Holy Spirit is the seeker and explorer of the depths of God. He is full of eyes, and what He finds, He reveals continually in the Son Jesus Christ. This aspect of His ministry is well personified in the four living creatures.

Their eyes within also give these angelic beings the ability to be full custodians of the inward light of Yeshua in other spirit beings. They are high energy spirits, whose inward and outward gaze can run to and fro across the cosmos, penetrating into the depths and the knowledge of the inward light of Christ within other spirit beings (angels). We could say that they are also a divine personification of the eyes of the Lord (2 Chronicles 16:9). They are watchers and stewards of the development of the different spectrums of the light of Christ within angels.

To embrace their ministry is to embrace the impartations of the knowledge of the glory of God. Our spirits were designed to be full of eyes that fully gaze and know Him who sits upon the throne.

In conclusion, our direct interaction with the angels from the first sphere is to bring us into a *mystical entanglement* with the Son. I would define this *"mystical entanglement"* as the experiential, direct pursuit of God that leads to a conscious, tangible union with Him. Those who follow this path of being mystically united with Jesus will interact with the angels of the first choir.

The seraphim of purity will cause one to become as a blowtorch, consumed by the fire of the love of God. Their fire separates by bringing one into the fellowship of the sufferings of the Christ. One cannot enter into union with the Son, Jesus Christ, without being in divine union with His sufferings and wounds. Few want to embrace and enter into union with His wounds.

The flaming sword, between the cherubim, judges and kills our *"soulish"* ways. And again, few want to leave their traditional lifestyles and embrace His cross. All that is of you and me has to be killed by the flaming sword, in order to let only Christ in us, minister before the ark, overshadowed by the cherubim, for only Jesus can minister between the ark. He alone entered into the most holy place once for all (Hebrews 9:12).

"I am crucified with Christ: nevertheless I live; yet not I, but Christ liveth in me: and the life which I now live in the flesh I live by the faith of the Son of God, who loved me, and gave himself for me." (Galatians 2:20)

The four living creatures will tutor us in the *art and the mystical lifestyle* of the way of the Tree of Life. This is a path that few have walked, for it is a path that becomes narrower and narrower, full of unopened treasuries and wet with many tears. It is both the road of bliss and our "'Via Dolorosa." It is both glorious celebrations and tears. It is the pathways of the sorrowing Christ and the pathways of the triumphant Christ. It is the exploration of the depths of His heart. It is the gleaning into the agony and the anguish of His heart, yet beholding the joys of a Savior's heart that has been raptured by the glance of His beloved.

The Angel(s) of the Lord

"In all their affliction he was afflicted, and the angel of his presence saved them: in his love and in his pity he redeemed them; and he bare them, and carried them all the days of old." (Isaiah 63:9)

"The angel of the LORD appeared to him in a blazing fire from the midst of a bush; and he looked, and behold, the bush was burning with fire." (Exodus 3:2-6)

All angels are angels of the Lord, but there seems to be a particular family of angels called the angel(s) of the LORD. These angels stand before His throne (Revelation 8:2). In Paul's letter to Timothy, he refers to them as the *'elect angels'* (1 Timothy 5:21).

The Lord does not have an angelic aspect of Himself or an expression of Himself as an angelic theophany. The Lord is the Lord of the angel armies, too grand to be compared to or put into the stream of the angelic.

"For unto which of the angels said he at any time, Thou art my Son, this day have I begotten thee? And again, I will be to him a Father, and he shall be to me a Son?" (Hebrews 1:5)

The angel of the Lord is not the Lord, nor a theophany of Jesus Christ. The term "angel of the Lord" represents different angels using that same title. The one that met Moses is not necessarily the one that Manoah met.

Peter had a personal angel, an angel who took his personal form when operating in this physical dimension (Acts 12:7). This angel would deputize on his behalf and do those things which his spirit man was capable of. Remember, our personal angels are only as strong as our spirit man is. And these angels, whose strength runs parallel to the growth of our spirit man, are surrogate angels. What the angel of Peter was to Peter, the angel(s) of the Lord is to the Lord.

Gabriel is part of this family of angels. Let us check out Zechariah's encounter with Gabriel:

"And there appeared unto him an angel of the Lord standing on the right side of the altar of incense." (Luke 1:11)

"And the angel answering said unto him, I am Gabriel, that stand in the presence of God; and am sent to speak unto thee, and to shew thee these glad tidings. And, behold, thou shalt be dumb, and not able to speak, until the day that these things shall be performed, because thou believest not my words, which shall be fulfilled in their season." (Luke 1:19-20)

One might wonder how come Luke calls him *"an* angel of the Lord," rather than *"the* angel of the Lord?" This is to show us that there is not just one angel of the Lord, but rather, it is an entire family..

In Exodus, Moses calls the angel that appeared to him, "The angel of the Lord." It seems like Moses is clearly distinguishing this angel as being the only one there is, but when Stephen the martyr recounts Moses' encounter, he says of the angel that appeared to Moses,

"And when forty years were expired, there appeared to him in the wilderness of mount Sina an angel of the Lord in a flame of fire in a bush." (Acts 7:30)

Stephen calls the angel "an angel of the Lord," as if to show us again that there are several angels of this calibre -- angels of the Lord.

These are a family of angels directly related to His throne room presence, as they stand much in the Shekinah presence of YHVH (Revelation 8:2). This is why Gabriel distinguishes himself from other angels by saying that He stands in the presence of God (Luke 1:19).

All angels stand and operate from within His presence, but certain angels have been granted the opportunity of being partakers of YHVH's *throne room* presence. These angels receive the lightnings of the glory of YHVH directly from the One Who sits on the throne.The angel(s) of the Lord have the capacity to seamlessly morph in and out of YHVH's direct hand of ministry. They carry the personal first narrative of YHVH that is in keeping with their created natures. We see this throughout the Old Testament, when the saints of old interacted with the angel(s) of the Lord. The angels' way of communicating sometimes takes YHVH's first person narrative and then sometimes comes out as though it's the angel speaking and not YHVH. The following scriptures bring great clarity:

"And the angel of the LORD called unto him out of heaven, and said, Abraham, Abraham: and he said, Here am I. And he said, Lay not thine hand upon the lad, neither do thou any thing unto him: for now I know that thou fearest God, seeing thou hast not withheld thy son, thine only son from me." (Genesis 22:11-12)

"Behold, I send an Angel before thee, to keep thee in the way, and to bring thee into the place which I have prepared. Beware of him, and obey his voice, provoke him not; for he will not pardon your transgressions: for my name is in him. But if thou shalt indeed obey his voice, and do all that I speak; then I will be an enemy unto thine enemies, and an adversary unto thine adversaries. For mine Angel shall go before thee, and bring thee in unto the Amorites, and the Hittites, and the Perizzites, and the Canaanites, and the Hivites, and the Jebusites: and I will cut them off." (Exodus 23:20-23)

The glories of YHVH that make up their spiritual composition is so great that one might not be able to discern between them and the Lord. The Lord literally fuses His word into these beings. They are high energy angels.

The angel(s) of the Lord are designed specifically to host a greater measure of the presence and revelations of the Lord. These are angels that YHVH embeds His character and nature in. The revelations of His character are manifested by the ministry of these angels. Through standing in His name and revealing the glories of His name, the angel(s) of the Lord have received a great name. YHVH also calls them the angel(s) of His presence.

Having received a much better name than the angels, He bestows upon them who believe on Him, a much better name, better than that of the angels; Jesus is the Greatest.

Chapter 5

The Second Sphere of Angels

The angelic hierarchy is based on the disposal and the flow of the revelations of God. The first sphere has a firsthand reception from God himself, then passes it down to the second sphere, and so on. This hierarchy has to do with the spiritual makeup of the angels, and every angelic sphere is a manifestation of a divine essence and source of Jesus Christ.

Every sphere is unique in its function and attributes. What we honor is not the position or the seat from whence the angel operates, but rather the graces and divine gifts of YHVH that have been lavishly formulated within the angel's spiritual makeup.

When Paul was expounding and explaining the majesty of Christ over all the nine spheres of the angelic hierarchy, he used the common Roman military terms to describe the celestial hierarchy. The names he attributed to the angelic hierarchy were names that showed the different functions of the then Roman authorities. The role of the Roman authorities in that era was similar to the role of the angels he attributed the name to.

Jesus' encounter with the man in the region of Gadarenes (Mark 5:1-10) gives us a glimpse at the use of Roman military terms to describe spiritual hierarchies. The possessed man identified himself based on a Roman military term. He called himself Legion, as there were thousands of demons inhabiting his body (Mark 5:9). In ancient Rome, a legion was a battalion of about three to six thousand soldiers.

He used a Roman title to describe who he was. Yet we know that demons predated Rome. What, then, was their name prior to Rome? I believe it was Legion.

Somehow, the fallen dominions, virtues, and principalities influenced Rome to name their military divisions after them. Remember, when the fallen angels rebelled, they retained their titles and powers.

Let us look at this according to ancient Roman mythology and religion. Mars was the god of war and the most prominent of the military gods in the Roman army. We know very well that Mars is not just a planet, but behind that planet is an angelic personification. This is the fallen angel Mars, who was worshipped as god of war in ancient Rome. He is most likely a fallen dominion.

This does not at all mean that the names of the angelic hierarchy are wrong or demonic; after all, our Lord Jesus Christ used the same Roman military terminology to describe His holy angels.

*"He said of them, Do you suppose that I cannot appeal to my father and he will immediately provide me with more than twelve **legions** of angels?" (Matthew 26:52)*

The names of the celestial hierarchy are those that denote and explain the corporate functions of the angels.

Dominions/Lordship

*"Far above all principality, and power, and might, and **dominion,** and every name that is named, not only in this world, but also in that which is to come." (Ephesians 1:21)*

I call Ephesians and Colossians the books of the supremacy of Christ over the angels. In the book of Ephesians, the Apostle named the second and third angelic hierarchy in their order and rank of authority, starting from the least.

The leaders of the second choir are dominions. They are lords in their essence, and they flow from the source of Jesus Christ as the Lord of lords. This sphere has to do mostly with the jurisdiction and operation of a lord. Under the dominions, we have the mighty ones, also known as virtues. The last in this sphere are the powers.

*"And the kingdom and **dominion**, and the greatness of the kingdom under the whole heaven, shall be given to the people of the saints of the most High, whose kingdom is an everlasting kingdom, and all **dominions** shall serve and obey him." (Daniel 7:27)*

In the later part of this book, I will mention some of the roles of the dominions, but I want us to look at the name Paul used in Ephesians.

Paul used the Greek word *kurios* to describe the dominions. This word was one given to a *master, a lord, and to a possessor and disposer of a thing.* It was a name attributed to someone who had power to decide.

The dominions are masters and they are lords over angelic households. They help in tutoring us and aiding us to function in the capacity of the Lordship of Jesus Christ. In possessing and disposing, they possess the authority of the Lord Jesus Christ and dispose it to other lesser angels. This they do by relaying God's *now* Word. They work closely with the first choir of angels.

Virtues, Mighty Ones, or Strongholds

*"Far above all principality, and power, and **might**, and dominion, and every name that is named, not only in this world, but also in that which is to come:"* *(Ephesians 1:21)*

The Greek word Paul used for mighty ones or virtues, when writing to the Ephesians was the word *dynameous.*

Dynameous in its Greek essence denotes inherent power, a power that is personified rather than one from an external source. This describes what the mighty ones are. These angels are an expression of the infinite virtues of YHVH in order to establish the realities of the Kingdom. They aid in maintaining the universe under the stream of the morality of YHVH. They are the manifestations of the rulership of His virtues.

In their general appearance, they are more like war horses (Zechariah 1:7-10). They carry and manifest the revelations of YHVH through their virtues. The virtues of YHVH are energies that reveal and establish the sweet tide of His rule over creation.

The virtues have these "virtues" as inherent power, releasing it and imparting it to other angels below them. In expressing the virtues of YHVH, they manifest the miraculous in the cosmos. They are pure strength; hence, that is why they are also called strongholds, and they impart this strength so that the miraculous rides upon the waves of YHVH's goodness.

We are told to seek the Kingdom of God and His righteousness (Matthew 6:33), for within His righteousness is a full manifestation of the ministry of the virtues. The righteousness of God is basically the right standing of God in a place which is an expression of heaven's culture or YHVH's attitude manifested. For instance, if there is chaos and turmoil in a place, what will be YHVH's attitude? It is to establish peace, and we know that peace is a virtue. So no matter how the peace is established, whether it is through divine provision, miracles, or just a sense of peace, a virtue is involved to some degree.

Powers/Authority

*"Far above all principality, and **power**, and might, and dominion, and every name that is named, not only in this world, but also in that which is to come:" (Ephesians 1:21)*

Let us take a look at the angels called powers. The word Paul used for powers is the Greek word *exousias*. This word denotes the sheer power and authority one has over **the body**.

I believe the *fallen powers* are the ones that regulate and watch over the possession of humans by demons.

In the kingdom of light, these are what I would call the harvesting angels, as these angels exert their power to influence humanity through angelic inspiration and nudges. They do this by releasing power and essences of their spiritual makeup to the angels below them, who operate on this earth. They also carry out the judicial decisions when it comes to the legal rights that the enemy may have in a life or place. They are also involved in spiritual warfare.

Powers are angels that wrestle with our wills, in order for us to bend with the tide of God's will. They are like re-routers. Yes, angels wrestle with us. They are also divine receptors and regulators of the divine power of YHVH. They flow from the Source of all power. Jesus Christ has been given all the power in heaven and on earth. These angels carry out judicial decisions when it comes to the legal rights that the enemy may have in a life or place.

Chapter 6

The Third Sphere of Angels

The last sphere consists of **principalities, archangels, and angels.** The angels in this sphere relate more to the earthly metacosm.

The *principalities* are princely angels or princes. They are under the manifestation of Jesus Christ as the Prince of princes, the Chief Prince of Peace. They conduct their acts in a princely fashion.

Michael is one of the few angels who closely resembles the pure manifestation of Jesus Christ as The Prince of princes, in higher degrees than other angels. I believe his strong and pure resemblance to Jesus' princely ministry allows him to morph and seamlessly flow into several offices. For instance, Gabriel calls Michael a great prince (Daniel 12:1), which is a name given to a principality, and Jude calls him an archangel (Jude 9). Since he carries a stronger depiction of the princely ministry of Yeshua, Michael is also an angel of the Lord; therefore, he is an angel of the Presence of the Lord.

In their functionality and mandate, principalities are overseers and governors over regions and territories, gatekeepers and watchers of the earthly nations.

The second in this sphere are the archangels. The archangels are the angels that link the principalities to the angels. They are the mighty connection link, overseeing the affairs of the earth. They are chief warring angels, doing battles on behalf of the saints and other angels.

Finally, we come to the last in the hierarchy, a family of spirit beings generally known as *angels*. The angels that we mostly find ministering in services and in our day-to-day lives are the "angels." This does not mean that they are inferior. They were created solely for that purpose. They are invaluable to humanity and they show up everywhere. Most times, they do not have wings.

Chapter 7

Understanding the
Realm of Visions

The first time our Lord speaks of the Kingdom to Nicodemus, He introduces him to an experiential Kingdom. God never presented an ethereal Kingdom to Nicodemus, nor to us. He said of the Kingdom,

*"Verily, verily, I say unto thee, Except a man be born again, he cannot **see** the kingdom of God." (John 3:3)*

The word used for sight there is the Greek word *horaó*, which conveys more than seeing. Rather, it denotes to experience, perceive, discern, and understand. Thus, it's a word that conveys a tangible knowing and perceptibility of the Kingdom realms.

The fall of the first Adam numbed men's perception of the realm of the spirit, and the resurrection of the second Adam awakened men's awareness of this realm. Jesus Christ has opened avenues and channels of our spirit man to experience, see, and hear into His Kingdom. I believe all of these avenues, which we will soon talk about, fall under the category of "visions."

When we talk of the realm of visions, the first thing that comes to our minds is "spiritual sight." The truth is that God's realm of visions should not just be limited to "seeing." Visions should rather be viewed as the climax point wherein our spiritual senses converge to experience, understand, and perceive the Kingdom of God. The end goal is to experience the knowable Christ and His Kingdom.

When the realm of heaven becomes visible or tangible in this dimension, it's called a vision. It is the point wherein our spirit man begins to vibrate in unison with the vibrations of heaven. This, in turn, brings a unified harmony between our faculties and heaven, enabling us to become one with heaven, partakers of heaven's nature.

This realm of visions is found within Him. The divine energies of His presence open up the realm of visions to us. But there is "The One" vision that leads to all other visions. This is the Vision of visions, and this is Jesus.

Jesus is the constant, perpetual, and ever expanding vision of YHVH. His face beheld is the breaking forth of the doorway into all visions.

Ezekiel makes an amazing statement:

"Now it came to pass in the thirtieth year, in the fourth month, in the fifth day of the month, as I was among the captives by the river of Chebar, that the heavens were opened, and I saw visions of God." (Ezekiel 1:1)

Ezekiel here says that he saw visions of God, but his first description of the "visions of God" is not necessarily YHVH himself. Ezekiel first describes the cherubim!

They are depths of the vision of the Father, which are the different facets of the image of the Son that reveals the Father and His household. We see the Son to see everything else.

Now, visions fall under three classifications: *inner* visions, *open* visions, and *closed* visions. Every class of visions has a positive, tangible effect on the body, soul, and spirit.

Inner visions have what I call inner feelings. These are the inward sensations of the Kingdom. These inward sensations usually do not numb us from our physical earthly sensations, so while I am having an inward experience of the Kingdom, my body still feels the effects of the room, the air, and atmosphere around me. When the inward sensations completely overwhelm my faculties, and I am totally wrapped up in them, I am entering into the fullness of a *horaó'*. A *horaó'* is the experience of the Kingdom as Jesus described it to Nicodemus. The word *horaó'* also means to inwardly experience and perceive. This is the place where the visions of God are seen, illuminated in the face of Jesus Christ.

From this place, we enter into what I have come to call open sensations, which are synonymous with open visions. This is the place where the sensations of the inward visions become outward, and your body no longer just has an inward awareness, but you also experience the sensations outwardly. Nevertheless, there is still a degree of external consciousness.

Then we have closed vision sensations. This is when all of your senses are immersed within heaven to the point that you lose touch or become unaware of physically interacting with the external world through your senses.

I have spoken first of the sensations of the three classes of visions because I want us to understand that the end goal of all visions is to perceive Him, to experience Him, and to understand that a vision is only a vision of God when divine essences, glories, and beauties of the Son break forth into one's soul. To experience and perceive the Son is what we were born for.

When we talk about experiencing Jesus, we mostly attribute it to our senses. The truth is that both the experience and the perceptibly of the Son comes through the *avenue* of our senses. This is the convergence and alignment of our entire being, zeroing in to know the Son.

If we look closely at both the Hebrew and the Greek words for visions, we will notice that they are two different words used to differentiate visions -- the words *chazon* and *marah* in the Hebrew Old Testament and the Greek words *optasia* and *horasis* in our New Testament. These words convey the depths of different degrees and manifestations in the realm of visions. Each vision within itself carries high energies and frequencies of God that would impact the growth of our spirit man in varying degrees. Not only do visions impact our spirit man, but they also open a doorway of the conscious tasting of the Christ, with the entire faculty of our being.

To fully understand the progression of visions in line with their Hebrew root meanings, let us look at Daniel. In Daniel 7:1, we are introduced to the first level of visions, generally known as inner visions, which are visions of the mind.

"...Daniel had a dream and visions of his head upon his bed."

Notice, Daniel says "visions of his head," hence these are visions that have to do with the imagination. This is the place where our imagination is illuminated and animated by the Holy Spirit to perceive into heaven through our thoughts or through the eyes of our heart. This can also be called "understanding to see" or "sight through understanding." It is the Lord awakening us on the inside so that we can see and perceive in the realm of the spirit through the "inner eye" and our thought faculties. This is very important, as training the eyes of our imagination allows us to enter into other depths and dimensions of visions, the *hazon* and the *marah*. Now, we find the word *hazon** in Daniel 8:16. This word means "to see, to behold." This word alludes to more of an "open vision" (seeing with the naked eyes) rather than a closed vision (trance-like state).

"And I heard a man's voice between the banks of Ulai, which called, and said, Gabriel, make this man to understand the vision." (Daniel 8:16)

The intensities of a *hazon* are greater than that of an inner vision, but a *hazon* is not the pinnacle of visions. In a *hazon*, our interactions with heaven have more of an earthly similitude. Here, Daniel said he heard the voice of a man, but that doesn't mean that the voice of the angel that spoke to Gabriel literally sounds like a man. In this *hazon*, the angel revealed himself in an earthly capacity, the reason being, the spirit of Daniel could only experience a *hazon* at that time. If you notice in Daniel 10, Daniel describes Gabriel in greater and more powerful detail. This is the same Gabriel he had seen in chapter 8. Had Gabriel changed? No, but rather Daniel's capacity to perceive heaven had changed. He had a *marah*.

The word used for vision in Daniel 10:8 is the Hebrew word *marah*. And he calls it a *great vision*, due to the intensities of the glories that were released. A *marah* is more of a trance. It is the point wherein the ecstasies of God envelope one to become raptured into a spiritual reality wherein all of the physical dimensions becomes ethereal. When you are in a trance, you are unconscious of the physical dimension. A trance not only affects the person in the trance but also those around. When Paul encountered the Lord on the road to Damascus, his companions fell off their horses. The spiritual energies that the trance released were that strong. This is one of the highest forms of spiritual impartation.

Encountering Found One (001)

It was almost dusk and the sky was turning into a dark, rich, velvety blue. The air was crisp, the little park pathway well lit with a golden yellow from the street lights. I wrapped my arms around my chest, trying to keep warm as the fall wind cut right through me. There appeared a man standing right in front of me who seemed to be in his mid 20s. He was wearing black jeans and a blue hoody. The front of his sweater was adorned with symbols and shapes that seemed other-worldly.

He was leaning against the street light, whistling into the night. As I approached, he suddenly stood in my way, not in an intimidating manner, but in a very friendly and welcoming way. To my amazement, I walked right through him.

I stopped dead in my tracks when the realization hit me... "You walked right through a man. This is not normal." I cautiously walked back to the individual and looked at him, but this time, I paid more attention to his facial features. He had the most perfectly trimmed black beard and hair that I had ever seen. He looked exactly like me, but a much more perfected version of me!

"Umm, Sir, you are not from this world, are you?" I respectfully asked. "People don't walk through other people in this world. It's not normal." He shook his head, smiling broadly. It was at this instance that I felt a strong presence of the Lord exuding from him. I was afraid, knowing he was divine. "No, I am not," he gently responded, assuring me that I was more than welcome to speak with him. "I know you!" I remarked. "You are my angel." He nodded and smiled.

"I am Found One, your angel, and I am here to take you to the house of Jesus. Come with me." I began to follow him, my body or spirit still feeling the strong effects of the presence of YHVH around him. While walking on the pathway, Found One stopped and spread his hands wide open into the air as if in worship. To my amazement, two books appeared before him hanging right in mid air, just between his wide open hands.

The first book was titled *The Book of the Mysteries of the Earth*. The second, I was not permitted to retain its title. Found One then looked at me and said, "The things that I am going to teach you are all written in these two books. Some of the things have been revealed to two men."

Spiritual attentiveness is the key for entering into an angelic encounter. With me, it was questioning how I had walked right through another man. With Moses, it was a bush that kept on burning. With you, it might be a bodily sensation, a continuous nudge, or unexplainable laughter. It might be lights flickering constantly from your peripheral vision. Heaven awaits your response, but what is the right attitude of responding?

Moses turned aside and moved closer to the bush, only to be told to take off his sandals. These sandals were made by the effort and sweat of human hands. Anything that has to do with human effort is not allowed to step on holy ground. The Lord required Moses' bare feet; the raw feet of a man, molded and made by YHVH's hands, without being covered by men's effort. That which has the essence of Adam the base earthly consciousness, molded from the tree of the knowledge of good and evil, cannot partake of heavenly realities. Moses' sandals were made by Adam's hands, and the Adam in all of us is religious to the core. It is through putting on the mind of Christ and allowing our Adamic earthly efforts to be eradicated that we fully enter into a conscious experience with heaven.

Understanding Spiritual Experiences

It is imperative that we do not try to limit spiritual experiences based on our natural insight. Our normal understanding of spiritual things can be subjective based on our theological filters, cultural background, and so on. We want to commit all understanding by standing under the superior knowledge of YHVH. The development of our threefold nature--spirit, soul, and body--plays an integral role as a divine catalyst to angelic encounters, visitations, and spiritual experiences. Knowing and understanding how the Light of heaven manifests in our life is the key to entering into spiritual experiences.

One of our personal responsibilities as children of God is the progressive development of our souls and the bringing of our physical bodies into subjection to the Lord. Subsequently, this causes the spirit man to supersede the functions of the flesh. The reason we don't experience the realm of the spirit as we would like to is that our flesh has not been completely over-ridden by our spirit man. By looking at the various stages of creation, we can see the full spectrum of God's desire and purpose in conforming men to His image and nature.

The creation of the earth gives us a fundamental insight into the manifestation of the spiritual realm into the physical. Let us follow closely the various stages and development of our earth in the first chapters of Genesis, and we will see the high note that was in God's heart for conforming His sons into His image.

Our bodies are approximately 70% water. The waters within our bodies bear record of our life. In Genesis, we find the Spirit of God hovering over the waters of the earth. The waters of the earth played a role of a mirror, through being a receptacle of the image and the heavenly frequencies of the Spirit. The Spirit vibrated over the waters of the earth to register within the memories of the earth the experiential knowledge and the intense frequencies of the energies of Christ. The earth was to have a memory and record that testified of its divine exposure to the vibrations of Him who dwells in unapproachable light. This testimony was to be an experiential testimony, for only then would the physical elements of the earth become familiar and vibrate with the frequencies of the energy of Jesus. When the waters of the earth had become familiar with the potency of the energies of the manifestation of Yeshua as the Light, YHVH spoke His Son: "Let there be light." Jesus was manifested as creative Light into the earth and its cosmos.

"And God said, Let there be light: and there was light." (Genesis 1:3)

"For That One was The Light of Truth, which enlightens every person that comes into the world." (John 1:9, Aramaic Version)

The earth saw fully into the Kingdom of our beautiful Jesus, because the Light of heaven had unveiled Himself to creation. So it is with us. Stillness in the presence of God is fundamental in changing the records held within the waters of our bodies. The presence of Yeshua will brood over us, causing our bodies to become tuned to the frequency of the manifestation of spiritual realms: visions, angelic encounters, trances, etc. This makes it easier for our spirits to overshadow our bodies. Our souls will be quickly raptured and triggered into His bliss, as the body now bears the record of the frequencies of a higher Kingdom.

Tuning into Spiritual Experiences

The veil between the natural and spiritual realms is a permeable membrane that we can enter into through spiritual perception. This dimension of heaven is experienced by those who possess a heavenly consciousness. We have angels around us all the time awaiting our interaction, and all it takes is a moment to tune our minds into our spiritual inheritance. By faith as a little child, knowing beyond knowing that we are not alone, let us entertain our heavenly friends.

I looked into thin air while soaking in the bathtub and began randomly trying to converse with angels. I did not see a thing, neither did I feel their presence. Speaking, "I love you guys, you are my buddies," I paid attention to the warmth in my heart as I felt the love of God swirl and illuminate the beauty of Jesus within me. It is the King within us who is the attraction for the angels. It is His presence gushing out from within that draws them. His face is the magnet for all of heaven.

At this moment, I perceived four angels in the bathroom. They had well-defined bodies like seasoned body builders; these were serious, strong, and mighty angels about seven feet tall. Excitedly, I said to them, "Where is Found One? I want to talk with him. Why do I hear his voice when I am alone, but seldom when preaching?" The other angels became excited and began to giggle as Found One stepped forward. He was serious and wearing a hooded garment. This time, his face had a white luminance. "Why so serious?" I asked. Without changing his expression, he said, "Reverence is the key that unlocks

74

the dimension of the realities of revelation." We cannot walk in the full manifestation of the revealed truth without reverence, neither can we receive the graces of revelation without reverence.

I noticed that Found One was carrying many different colored scrolls. Seeing that I paid attention to the scrolls, he said to me, " These are yours."

"Why haven't you given them to me before?" I asked. "I am always here. I miss your voice."

With authority and calm, he said, "You have to come into my dimension to receive them." What does it mean to enter into the dimension of the angels? To fully know someone, you have to consciously live in their environment, and to receive heaven, you have to be in its atmospheres. Since we have been born into this earth, we understand earth's environment and we live and breathe the oxygen of this earth. We have learned how to be sustained by the principles of this earth. To know and understand heaven, we have to live a life vibrating with the frequencies of heaven. This allows us to transcend above earthly consciousness into the realms of heaven. To vibrate at the frequencies of heaven requires us to live by every word or sound that proceeds from the mouth of YHVH. His breath is the oxygen of heaven by which we are sustained and nurtured. This is the environment in which we will be re-educated, renewed, and be fully immersed in the dimensions of the Lord of Hosts. These are the dimensions of the angelic canopy, the spiritual universe of YHVH.

The revelations of YHVH are received by those who have made the spiritual universe of YHVH their habitation.

"I was in the Spirit on the Lord's day, and heard behind me a great voice, as of a trumpet." (Revelations 1:10)

God has revelations of Himself specifically designed to be ushered into this cosmos by our individual spirit man. We are uniquely designed to be mobile schools of His revelations and wisdom.The entire creation awaits the revealed sons who will bring the sound of YHVH's voice into the cosmos. The offspring of YHVH are to make known His manifold wisdom to the rulers and authorities in the heavenly realms (Ephesians 3:10). But we have to consciously ascend into this realm. Heaven awaits us. Let us ascend, oh sons of God!

"And he put forth the form of an hand, and took me by a lock of mine head; and the spirit lifted me up between the earth and the heaven, and brought me in the visions of God..." (Ezekiel 8:3)

"We Have Come To Impart"

The anointing was gently settling upon and within me. It had been ten minutes since I had been praying in tongues. I was hanging out with a friend of mine, a well seasoned seer. He said to me, "You were calling and instructing your angels, and they are here to impart." I had not seen much up to now, just little flickers of light here and there. I was quite excited. The atmosphere was charged with the expectation of what the Lord was about to do. I walked into the center of our living room, my face gleaming with childlike faith. My friend gestured me to stretch out my hands as if to receive something. "Michael, there are two angels with you. One is in front and one is behind you. Rest your spirit, be calm and relaxed," he said. I did so as a steady awe settled upon me.

Why the steadying and calming of one's soul for an angelic impartation? you may ask. Simply because God does not touch moving objects. It's our responsibility to silence *the noises* of our soul by focusing our gaze upon Jesus. The impartations of God are stronger when we are resting in Him. God touches us fully when we lean our restless souls (which are in turmoil apart from Him) into the sweet tide of His steady and refreshing waves of divine bliss. I was not at all prepared for what took place next.

I closed my eyes and stretched out my hands, feeling like a giant mushy marshmallow. Two hands pressed right into me like fire, one from the back and the other from the front. They penetrated right through my soul and into my spirit man. I felt the separation of my body, soul, and spirit and entered into the conscious reality of a tripartite being. My soul was churning as my spirit man separated itself from the ungodly pull of the soul. This was the beginning of my ability to see into the spirit. The soul had been violently moved and made way for my spiritual retina. My spirit man could now see into the Kingdom realms of YHVH without the distractions and blockages from my soul. I experienced what Paul meant when he said,

"...piercing even to the dividing asunder of soul and spirit, and of the joints and marrow, and is a discerner of the thoughts and intents of the heart." (Hebrews 4:12)

Our souls can be molded and shaped either after that which is external or internal. We are spirit beings who have been given a soul which has an intermediary function, connecting two realms. One of the processes of growth as sons of God is to learn to separate the spirit from the soul. The spirit is the faculty of our being which navigates and explores the spiritual world in union with Christ, Who is the Door. The soul also is supposed to register, store, and allow the revelations and impartations received by the spirit to be administered into this physical world. The soul bridges the spiritual and the physical. Problems arise when the soul embeds itself with our spirit instead of allowing divine life to flow out. This clogs our spiritual senses, and the soul, instead of bridging the spiritual to the physical, now acts as a bridge of the physical to the spirit man. Thus, we live from the outside in, instead of from the inside out.

The spirit man now becomes mindful of that which is physical and temporal. Our souls and our spirits have to be split for our spirit man to fully experience heavenly realities and for the rivers of heaven to have free flow from heaven to earth.

Chapter 8

Understanding
Visitations and
Encounters

We need to establish that the key to all visitations and encounters should flow from a place of deep abiding intimacy with God. We need to encounter and experience Him through a direct interaction with His presence. Within His abiding presence is the doorway into all manifestations. There is no real manifestation of the angelic canopy outside of His presence. All of heaven is in awe of Him, and all of heaven is built upon the networking and interaction of all beings around the person of the Lord Jesus Christ.

There is a need to differentiate between an angelic encounter and a visitation. Though they may sound alike, they are not necessarily the same. Not all encounters with angels are visitations, and most visitations can be referred to as encounters, but they are a higher form of encounter. I would define an angelic encounter as a manifestation of angelic beings that are already present in a place that you intentionally turn into and engage with. Encounters can be self-triggered, either during worship or through an intentional desire to turn full on into the Kingdom realities.

Visitations have to do with God's timing, as well as the progressive growth of your spirit man, blended together with desire. An angelic visitation occurs when an angel is sent from the Father in an ambassadorial capacity with a message, proclamation, or assignment. It usually means that there is a change of the season or something new taking place in the earth or one's life. These are often scary encounters. Visitations are also more formal and leave branded within the souls of men a greater depth of the revelation of Jesus Christ. They come with stronger spiritual energy, impartations, and a higher degree of the fear of the Lord. These angels are coming fresh from the presence of Him who is Lord of all.

You can encounter your personal angels right now, by practicing your sight. The Scriptures encourage us to practice our spiritual senses. Again, I say, by virtue of being born from above, as believers seeing into the realm of the spirit is our inheritance.

How, then, can we live in a place of encountering our personal angels? Desire is a key that unlocks doors in the realm of the spirit.

Desire must first be anchored within the heart of the Father from whom all good things flow. It is His desire and good pleasure to give us the Kingdom. Our desire to engage with angels must flow from a platform of love, honor, and humility. It is imperative that our desire be filled with childlike wonder at our heavenly Father's joy that we should engage with His angels. He is the Lord of Hosts.

Initially, when I wanted to engage with the angels of the Kingdom of our Father, I would quiet my soul and simply ask the Lord to show me where the angels were in the room. I would eventually begin to perceive that I was not alone. I would continue to ask the Lord for guidance, like a child being taught by his dad. Sometimes, it would be like light, transparent, or sometimes very visible. Sometimes, the angels would look like flashes of light flitting about the room or like light orbs.

By looking and observing, divine impartations of the sweetness of heaven's bliss would be transferred from them to me. Almost always, the atmosphere would change and the place would become fraught with the tangible presence of Yahweh as I would begin to feel His presence bodily. I would ask the angel his name, audibly or by thought, and usually I would then begin to understand his function. Sometimes, his very appearance expresses his name and function.

Honor is a large part of engaging with the angels. Our Father has assigned angels to us to walk with us throughout our lives as our personal angels--for various events, for ministry, and a host of other things. Honor looks like saying hello and even saying thank you. This takes practice and discipline. Discipline soon becomes a delight as interaction with the angels becomes a normal part of our lives.

Triggering Angelic Visitations

"And He saith unto him, Verily, verily, I say unto you, Hereafter ye shall see heaven open, and the angels of God ascending and descending upon the Son of man." (John 1:51)

This simple yet profound statement of our King to Nathaniel, "Hereafter ye shall see heaven open, and the angels of God ascending and descending upon the Son of man," has made me wonder why Jesus said that the angels first ascended before they descended to Him? In the normative, everyday sense, angels, whose abode is in heaven, should be first descending from heaven to earth. I believe Jesus was showing us the key to triggering angelic visitations.

An angelic visitation, which is an authorized *descent* of an angel into this realm, first begins with angels ascending. Visitations are triggered and put into motion through an angelic ascension. Those who have learned to live in an ascended state in the Kingdom realms of YHVH have this dimension of angelic visitations opened to them in a higher degree. This ascension of angels is stimulated and orchestrated by the conscious position of one's spirit man in the Kingdom realms. Thus, the spirit has to be seated in heavenly places in Christ Jesus.

We are spirit beings who have a soul and live in a body. Our intricate tripartite makeup is so designed to allow us to be able to live in two worlds: the spiritual and the physical. So, we are trans-dimensional beings with the ability to live multi-dimensionally, that is, in the physical realms and the spiritual realms. The abode of the spirit man was meant to be in the heavenly places where Christ is seated, and the abode of the body is relatable to this earth to function within it. The soul that connects the spirit to the body was to bridge and create a convergence between our spirit man sitting in heavenly places and our bodies in this natural or earthly realm. Therefore, by virtue of the design of our bodies, we are to be a constant bridge of heaven to earth and earth to heaven. Remember, *us abiding in Christ* enables us to enter into the conscious experience of heaven, and *Christ in us* allows us to consciously bring heaven's domain into this earthly cosmos.

When Yeshua spoke to Nathaniel, He clearly demonstrated that the angels are *descending and ascending* unto Him. Wherever they are *ascending* to, they are *ascending* to Jesus, and wherever they are *descending* to, they are *descending* to Jesus—simultaneous dwelling of Jesus, the Son of man who is on earth and also in heaven.

The scriptures clearly say that YHVH has translated us into the Kingdom of His dear Son (Colossians 1:13). The word *translate* here implies a change in a spirit being's environment. As much as our bodies are locally in this earth realm, our spirit man is in heavenly places. In Jesus Christ, we have entered the realm and realities of being multi-present. What does being in two realms have to do with angels ascending to us, before they descend?

When we are born into this world, the love of Father that is lavished upon us enables angels to be assigned to us. These are what we have grown to know as our guardian angels. These angels are there to influence and guide us into our God-given purposes. Their promptings in our lives are only as strong as our spirit man. Our guardian angels have been present since we were born, but their service is fully triggered and put into full motion when they ascend and receive instruction from our spirit man. To allow this to happen, we need to enter into the glorification of Jesus Christ through a genuine born again experience. Without being born again, our spirit man is earthy, and its influence and functionality is contained within this temporal world.

Entering the glorification of Jesus allows us to be partakers of His divine nature, hence we also become the sons of God on earth and in heaven. If we remain earthy and under the frequencies of this earthly cosmos, there is no need for angels to ascend to the place where our spirit man is supposed to be seated in Christ Jesus.

The glory of Christ translates our spirit man into heavenly places. Now our spirit man, through entering the glorification of Jesus, becomes mindful of that which is heavenly, since its surroundings and its new place of abode is heaven. The *soul* now needs to be mindful and set its gaze upon that which is heavenly. The reality of where we are seated, in Christ Jesus, has to envelop the consciousness of our souls in this earth realm. This creates a ladder that establishes a constant flow of angels, ascending to that place where they can receive instructions from our spirit man, and then descending to us. Angels grow in strength, as well, and the power of their functionality, service, and aid in our lives increases when they ascend to our spirit man in heavenly places.

Angels are subject to our spirit man, as they are spirit beings. Spirit beings relate to spirit beings. They receive instruction and mandates from our spirit man in union with the Holy Spirit. Jesus has placed our spirit man with Him, at the right hand of the Father, so our angels need to ascend to that place before they descend into this physical realm. They are ascending, because they firstly descended to us as gifts from the Father when we were physically birthed.

This is what Jesus meant when He said "ascend first." The angels can only ascend if our spirit man and soul have a mutual consciousness of heaven. Thus, the soul needs to mirror that which the spirit man in heaven is partaking of, to create "Jacob's ladder" or rather, "Michael's ladder." Paul urges us to

"Set your affection on things above, not on things on the earth." (Colossians 3:2)

Chapter 9

Desiring Spiritual Realities

"*To the degree that you hold something intimately in your heart, you can enter into its reality. Desire is the key.*" (*Anonymous*)

"*I knew a man in Christ above fourteen years ago, (whether in the body, I cannot tell; or whether out of the body, I cannot tell: God knoweth;) such an one caught up to the third heaven.*" (*1 Corinthians 12:2*)

"*After these things I saw, and behold, a door opened in Heaven, and a voice which I heard like a trumpet speaking with me saying, 'Come up here, and I shall show you whatever is granted to happen after these things.'*" (*Revelations 4:1, Aramaic Version*)

"*God is a Spirit: and they that worship him must worship him in spirit and in truth.*" (*John 4:24*)

"*Whereby are given unto us exceeding great and precious promises: that by these ye might be partakers of the divine nature, having escaped the corruption that is in the world through lust.*" (*1 Peter 1:24*)

"*And he put forth the form of an hand, and took me by a lock of mine head; and the spirit lifted me up between the earth and the heaven, and brought me in the visions of God.*" (*Ezekiel 8:3*)

One of the most important truths we need to fully embrace is the fact that we are born into a Kingdom of spirits, which requires spiritual people to engage with it. We need to have a spiritual consciousness to operate in the Kingdom of God.

To be spiritually conscious, we must be intentional, as the scripture tells us to set our affections on that which is above and think about that which is heavenly.

If we continue to intentionally shift our mindsets to heavenly things and we begin to see ourselves as in this world but not of it, then we would be coming into agreement with the words of Jesus to see the reality of the scripture "as a man *thinks* in his heart so is he" (Proverbs 23:7).

As new creation beings, it should be absolutely normal for us to engage with our homeland. The heavenly realms is our spiritual birthplace. Jesus has made us spirit beings, literal citizens of heaven, but our Adamic mindsets need to be renewed into the mind of Jesus. Hence, the consciousness of Adam in us has to be eradicated. We need a heavenly consciousness!

The more we give honor to the things of the spirit, the more we will see it open up to us. It is possible to live a life that is continuously conscious of the unseen realms. We must be aware of heaven in order for our perception to change. All it takes is putting on the mind of Christ, for the Kingdom belongs to spiritual people who have the mind of Christ.

Angels are heavenly beings who are attracted to the frequencies of heaven; therefore, the data in our minds is important. Our thought patterns release frequencies, either earthly or heavenly. Heaven only reveals itself to him who is heavenly.

"He that cometh from above is above all: he that is of the earth is earthly, and speaketh of the earth: he that cometh from heaven is above all." (John 3:31)

A heavenly person speaks of heavenly things and consciously knows that he is seated in heavenly places in Christ Jesus. The earthy Christian is more mindful of this physical realm, and to him, heaven is a place that awaits his transition from earth via his death. The realm of angels is a distant reality to the earthy Christian. He *hopes* for a futuristic heavenly reality.

God has not called us to a Gospel of hope alone. He has called us to the experiential Christ in whom we experience all Kingdom realities.

"If in this life only we have hope in Christ, we are of all men most miserable." (1 Corinthians 15:19)

Hope is good, but hope alone is not good. I don't just want to hope for the realities of heaven. I want to walk in heavenly realities. No more merely hoping for a futuristic, *"death sweep me into heaven"* reality.

By faith, I step into my inheritance as a son of God. By faith, I embrace the fact that I am a spirit being.

I am a spirit being with a soul, housed in a body. I have the mind of Christ. My consciousness is flooded with the light of the Living Christ. My mind is illuminated to understand heavenly things, for I am a heavenly man. I see angels; I have trances, visions, and spiritual experiences. I function as a spirit, as I am the offspring of YHVH Who is a spirit.

It is prison break time! Let us break free from the shackles of the Adam in us, which is the greatest prison there is. Let us break free from the confinement and tethering to the physical rudiments of this earth. We are living light beings, we are sons of God and sons of men. We must refuse to be trapped in the realm of this earth.

Let us embrace the fact that we are the revelation of YHVH to this cosmos. Let's get on it!

Understanding Our Heavenly Nature

We have already established that angels are spirit beings living in a spiritual dimension. Since these angelic beings relate with spirits, it is critical that we know our heavenly nature.

The Holy Spirit is the Chief Spirit whose desire is that all spirits under Him may relate one to another in an honoring family manner. He is not just our seal, He is also the awakener and the resurrector of our spirits. One of the reasons He energizes and awakens the faculties of our spirit man is so we can relate to other spirits in a more coherent way. Positive and beneficial relationships between spirits are at the core of His heart. But how can one spirit benefit from another spirit, if the other doesn't fully know its identity as a spirit being?

Since it takes spirits to fully relate with spirits, Jesus had to go to the cross to create infinite possibilities of such relationships.

His death and resurrection established one sea of spirits within Himself -- a divine relationship between sons and angels; spirit beings who can relate with each other. Paul writes a powerful word in Colossians 1:20:

*"And, having made peace through the blood of his cross, by him to reconcile **all things** unto him; by him, I say, whether they be things in earth, or things in heaven."*

The *reconciliation* was the bridging together of all spirit beings around the pleasures of Jesus Christ. Jesus is the "Eden" of YHVH, who bridges all creations together by the pleasures of His Person. Angels and sons are bridged and inter-connected together through the realm of enjoying Jesus. His pleasures are what knit spirits together with spirits.

The Holy Spirit showed me another scripture:
*"But now you are in Yeshua The Messiah, when from the first you were distant, and you have come near by the blood of The Messiah. For he is our peace **who made the two one, and he destroyed the wall that was standing in the middle.** And he has canceled the hatred by his flesh and the law of commands in his commandments, that for the two, he would create in his Person one new man, and he has made peace. And he has reconciled the two with God in one body, **and in his crucifixion he has killed the hatred.** And he came preaching The News of Peace to you, to the distant ones and to those who are near, Because in him, we both have access by One Spirit to The Father." (Ephesians 2: 13-17)*

This scripture *not only* talks about the wall of separation between the Jew and the Gentile, as it has been taught. The Holy Spirit caused me to read this scripture in context to spirits, the Jew being the heavenly realm and its spirits that did not fall, the Gentile being all of Adam and this earthly cosmos, and the wall of partition being the sin nature that kept us from interacting legally with the spiritual dimension.

Jesus has reconciled the physical realms and the spiritual realms in Himself, as it was before the fall. In Jesus, there is neither Jew nor Gentile, neither spirit nor physical, for we are all spirits in Christ Jesus. To the Christian, there should be no separation between the two, but an intermingling of two worlds and dimensions, Eden and earth together!

We now consciously have the full rights of spirit beings, no more barred from Eden, and we should no longer view ourselves as base fallen man. We are sons of the Great Spirit of YHVH!

The "one new man" He created in His Person is a divine union of relationship between heaven and earth, entering into the inheritance of heaven and being enveloped by its essences. Thus, earth conforms into heaven and through this, enters into oneness with heaven. And by earth, I mean the physical man. The *one new man* is also the establishment of communion between spirits born of His light and spirits that bring His light of servitude, man and angels, co-relating together because they are spirit beings. The ultimate Son Jesus Christ did it all!

The partition wall has been destroyed and the spiritual dimension has been opened, so that as spirit beings, we can become fully immersed into the spheres of heaven. It is fundamental that we know our spiritual makeup in order to fully relate with our new environment.

One day, the Holy Spirit said clearly to me in the shower, "You are not Moses' tabernacle, neither are you any other man's tabernacle. You are Michael Aviel's tabernacle!"

The tabernacle that Moses built was a heavenly reflection of Moses' servanthood ministry that required strict ritualistic regulations and observations for one to enter into the Holy of Holies. It was the physical expression of the ministry that Moses' spirit man was establishing and bringing Israel into.

"Then verily the first covenant had also ordinances of divine service, and an earthly sanctuary." (Hebrews 9:1)

In Christ, there are no earthly sanctuaries, only heavenly. Hear what Paul says concerning the Christ tabernacle, which we are:

*"But Christ being come an high priest of good things to come, **by a greater and more perfect tabernacle,** not made with hands, that is to say, not of this building..." (Hebrews 9:11)*

"In whom ye are also are builded together for an habitation of God through the Spirit." (Ephesians 2:22)

"For Christ has not entered into the holy places made with hands .. but into Heaven itself." (Hebrews 9:24)

Moses' tabernacle was earthly, as Moses was Adamic. None of us are Moses' tabernacle. We are heaven personified, for we are born in the image of heaven Himself, Jesus, the Heaven of heavens. The structure of our threefold nature is totally different from the accepted notion of outer court, inner court, and Holy of Holies. Our entire spiritual makeup is totally different. We are being molded into His image. He is one nature, the Most Holy.

We are sons being built as living stones, not made with the tent-like material which Moses used to build his tabernacle. Tents signify a nomadic lifestyle, a constant life of camping in one region or another. A house of living stone signifies a resting place, a permanent place of abode for God. YHVH has found a resting place, in His houses of living stones being built for the living Christ, Who is the Chief Cornerstone.

Jesus is our mirror, and He has no partitions of separation; He has no inner court, outer court, and Holy of Holies. In Him, we see the personification of holiness. He is the God-man whose outer, inner, and Holy of Holies is the most Holy. It is His desire that our entire tripartite being should be flooded with His holiness. This is transfiguration, our conscious knowing and walking as living light spirit beings.

The Spirit Man and His Relation to Angels

The spirit of a man is his pure raw identity. As the physical body carries blood, so the spirit has veins, ligaments, and organs that carry blood. This blood is that of YESHUA, translated as His light if we are born of Him. Within this light is YHVH'S blueprint for our individual lives. This blueprint is the revelations of the Faces of God that our spirit man is to usher into this cosmos and by which we are to live in response to.

Jesus has put His Kingdom within the realms of our spirit man. The scripture tells us that of the increase of His Kingdom there shall be no end; hence, if the expanse of an endless kingdom is within us, that means that the spirit man is an ever increasing phenomenon. Our spirit man can become as infinite as the universe and as minute as an atom. It is the faculty of our being that operates in the realms of the *Now*. It is in I AM, beyond the confinement of time and space. It transcends the physical properties of this physical dimension.

Since the physical properties do not define it, the spirit of a man born of Christ operates trans-dimensionally. There are moments in meetings where I have expanded my spirit man to cover the entire meeting, allowing the glory of the Lord to become the overshadowing of the people. You can expand your spirit man to cover and brood over your entire city!

The reason we do not see the vast operation of our spirit man is because most of its faculties are still sleeping and need to be awakened by the perpetual energizing of the Holy Spirit. This is one of the reasons we are baptized with the Spirit. The Holy Spirit is the source of all constructive energy in the Kingdom, and we receive supplies of energy from the realities we turn to. The scriptures tell us that if we sow to the flesh, we will reap from the flesh, and if we sow to the spirit, we will reap from the spirit. The awakening of certain aspects of our spirit man means that angels that stand and function in that particular aspect can now work with us.

There are various divisions and ministry of angels to us. Remember that one of the reasons they minister to us is to reveal to us a particular aspect and operation of our spirit man. This, in turn, allows us to have the God-given authority to relate and to instruct them. We see this perfect example with David in Psalms 103:20.

"Bless the LORD, ye his angels, that excel in strength, that do his commandments, hearkening unto the voice of his word."

The Holy Spirit does not directly instruct the angels to worship Him. We see the Spirit has delegated that responsibility to the psalmist! David clearly illustrates that he has the authority to instruct *worshipping angels.* This is because the faculty of his spirit man that relates to YHVH through worship has been awakened and energized.

Relating to angels runs parallel to the awakening of the faculties of our spirit man. We have attributes of our spirit man that are awaiting to be awakened, so that angels who stand in those attributes can be employed and put to service. But how are the faculties of our spirit man awakened? By the WORD of GOD, Jesus Christ alone. He awakens the faculties of our spirit man that are asleep. The scriptures say,

"Marvel not at this: for the hour is coming, in the which all that are in the graves shall hear his voice." (John 5:28)

I believe that the hearing of His voice is also speaking to the awakening of the faculties of our spirit man that still live in a "grave-like state." When the voice of the Father is unveiled through the glory of His presence to reveal the living individual Christ Jesus, then the awakening of the faculties of our spirit man takes place.

Understanding Spiritual Energies

The angelic canopy is a sort of hierarchy based on mandate and assignments. It is based on how close the angels are to the throne of God. The closer the angel is to YHVH's throne room presence, the stronger the angel. This is because YHVH's throne is a place were high energy impulses of His person are released to creation.

There are angels that are firsthand partakers of the energy of God from His throne. In most cases, these angels carry such high intensities of the presence of God that one might not be able to discern between them and the Lord.

Jesus has set our hearts as His throne. The energies of the Throne of YHVH within us have to be released in order for our spirit man to be built. Our guardian angels usually operate to the capacity of the strength of our spirit man. That is why, in most cases, one person might have a greater demonstration of a certain gift than another. (*As you will see later on, a spiritual gift is synonymous with an angel.*) **12**

The presence of the Lord, as much as it is the manifestation of the person of the Lord Jesus Christ, is also the energy by which all the activities of God in the spiritual realm are accomplished. We need to constantly turn inwards and allow the person of the Holy Spirit to energize us from the inside out. This will result in more manifestations and activations of our personal angels, as the glories from within His throne in our hearts is imparted to the angels.

"Now unto him that is able to do exceeding abundantly above all that we ask or think, according to the power that works in us." (Ephesians 3:20)

The Greek word "power" in this verse refers to not just physical power, but to energy. It is the word *energizo*, from which we get the word "energy."

As much as our spirit man is our pure identity, it is also the faculty of our being that possesses the power of God. This energy is the one through which miracles are wrought in the name of Jesus. When the scriptures say *"edifies* your spirit" (1 Corinthians 14:4), the edification is also learning to allow the essential flow of the "currents" of God within us. The edification can be defined as the empowerment and the building up of our spirit man by the person of the Holy Spirit.

The Holy Spirit lives within our spirit and is the One by Whom we are able to minister the power of God. Around the faculty of our spirit is a "shell," that functions as a cage, that confines or disallows the energy of the Holy Spirit. This shell, which is our soul, must be cracked open for the Light of the living Christ to be made manifest.

As long as "soulish" ways are dominant in an individual's life, the soul will act as a cage or cell to restrict the full flow of the power of God. Learning to deal with issues which are blockages in one's soul will enable one to know how to navigate through the energies of God. Our guardian angels need impartations of the energies of God from within us.

The works of miracles are not individually done; they require and always have angelic aid. The angels receive the energies from within us, as we are energized in His presence. This energy of the person of the Holy Spirit is not just a raw constructive energy, but within its essence is embedded the *Rhema* word of God.

The *WORD* that is encoded within this energy carries the purpose and reason why it is being imparted to the angels. All energy comes from Him who is *THE LIGHT*. Light is pure energy, but all forms of the light of Yeshua have different purposes. For instance, the light for working miracles carries within its brilliant spectrum the spoken word for the kind of miracles that an angel is to bring to the people to whom we are ministering.

Chapter 10

Beautiful Holy Spirit and His Gifts

'*B*ut the **manifestation of the Spirit** *is given to every man to profit withal. For to one is given by the Spirit the word of wisdom; to another the word of knowledge by the same Spirit; to another faith by the same Spirit; to another the **gifts of** healing by the same Spirit; to another the working of miracles; to another prophecy; to another discerning of spirits; to another divers kinds of tongues; to another the interpretation of tongues: But all these worketh that one and the selfsame Spirit, dividing to every man severally as he will."* (1 Corinthians 12:7-11)

The workmanship of God is through living beings, who have been specifically crafted for a particular mandate. Paul the apostle, in his letter to the Corinthians, writes about spiritual gifts. These gifts themselves are synonymous with angels, as the gift comes packaged with its assigned angel.

When the Lord deposits spiritual gifts to an individual, an angel or spirit being that functions in that office is given to work with that individual. The *gift* usually comes as the power or authority to relate seamlessly with that angel. All of the nine gifts of the Holy Spirit have angels that aid us in their operation. One could say that to a certain degree, the angel is the gift. For example, when the scriptures say, *"...and the power of the Lord was present to heal them"* (Luke 5:17), it is not talking about some raw abstract power, but an angel of power was present to execute the healing.

There is a beautiful, flowing relationship between the Holy Spirit and angels. The manner in which the person of the Holy Spirit coordinates His nature through and by the angels is spectacular. The Holy Spirit's meek nature is one of servitude. He is the Spirit of Christ and the crown of the Holy Spirit is the crown of servitude. The angels are ministering spirits and they live and operate in the shadow of the glorious light of this crown of humility. Even the grooves, channels, or veins (for lack of a better term) within the spiritual composition of the angels are so designed that they reflect and receive the energies that carry frequencies of humility and servitude. The bond that binds all this together is a beautiful attitude of preferring one another. Giving preference to one another is an integral core and protocol of heaven's atmosphere. Heaven is family-oriented, rooted in honor, and each spirit being's desire is for the other.

The very heart of heaven reflects the servanthood nature of YHVH, so these ministering spirits also embody and manifest the humble nature of our servant King.

The Bible says, "... as He is, so are we in this world" (1 John 4:17), so to fully know how to work with angels, we need to understand how the Holy Spirit relates to the angels in the most coherent, loving, family way. These selfless spiritual beings are drawn more to an individual whose heart reflects the nature of Christ since they readily respond to the Living Word Himself. It was an angel who said to John G. Lake, in response to a waning revival, *"Human selfishness and human pride have consumed and dissipated the very glory and heavenly power that God once gave from heaven to this movement as you have beheld tonight."* The scriptures express this principle:

"God resists the proud and gives grace to the humble." (1 Peter 5:5-6)

If The Holy Spirit, Why Angels?

The Holy Spirit is the Kingdom of YHVH personified, and He is the Kingdom of YHVH manifested. So all activities happen in the Kingdom under His light. We are all literally swimming in the vast, endless, and bottomless ocean called the Holy Spirit, if we are born of Him. As A.W. Tozer once said, "our God is a shoreless sea of pleasure."

"For in Him we live, and move, and have our being." (Acts 17:28)

"If we walk in the light, as he is in the light, we have fellowship one with another, and the blood of Jesus Christ his Son cleanseth us from all sin." (1 John 1:7)

As much as all activities are in Him and infused by Him, I believe that the dearest thing in His heart is to fully prepare Mrs. Jesus Christ. He is the purifying fire within us. He is the fiery love of the Father manifested in and through our lives.

It took me about six months to begin to understand and enter into the reality of the words that an angel had spoken to me: "Michael, haven't you learned all this time that Yeshua has been looking for simply a lover in you?" Not a worker, not a servant, not a preacher, but just someone with whom He can have intimate, heart-to-heart exchange.

Lovers cherish intimacy, and the communication and interaction between us and the Holy Spirit primarily has to do with intimacy. Thus, His voice, in most cases (but not always) is to woo us and whisper the "*lovey dovey*" sweet intentions. He is concerned about that inward relationship with Him, whereas most anything that happens externally has to do with angelic activity.

The speaking and interaction of us with the angels has to do with function, purpose, and mandate. They are servants of YHVH, and most of their conversations are to elevate us into the realms of Kingdom operation. An angel will not lead us into intimacy, but will assist us to fully function in the works of YHVH.

A man can walk in amazing angelic activity, but knowing the Lord of the hosts comes as a result of the inward gaze of the soul upon Him. By virtue of "noising oneself" to God, i.e externally praying loudly, one can receive an anointing and walk in an outward demonstration of power. This is a result of networking with angels, but YHVH is known though the inward descent of the soul, which leads to a face-to-face communion with Him. One can know Kingdom functions without intimacy, because functionality comes as a result of interacting with angels.

First Corinthians 13 outlines an outward demonstration of power one can walk in without love. Most things outlined by Paul in 1 Corinthians 13 are external workings of the Holy Spirit, which are acts of angels. He, the Holy Spirit, is the One who initiates the workings of angelic activities.

In this chapter, St. Paul is not merely speaking on a surface level. He is saying that we can know mysteries, do miracles, speak with tongues of men and angels, which leads to angelic visitations, yet not have intimacy with God. The love that Paul is talking about is the person of the Lord Jesus Christ Himself, not some temporal burst of emotion. Paul is saying that we can walk in all these things without an intimate love exchange and fellowship with Jesus Christ, who is Love personified.

The child of that intimate relationship is Love itself, as outlined in 1 Corinthians 13. Intimacy with Jesus births love. Love then makes its personification in us. We don't have to force ourselves to love, because love is a natural outflow of being in an intimate love relationship with the Lord. The church at large thinks that because we can feel "goose bumps," "bodily sensations," and "winds" around us, we have intimacy with Jesus. This is angelic activity around us. Intimacy, in most cases, begins with the stillness of the soul and the turning away from all external interactions to gaze upon His indescribable beauty. We are also required to know the workings of the Father. Knowing how He operates will result in increased angelic interaction.

There are two aspects of the Bride: intimacy and responsibility. Intimacy is the deep enjoyment of our Beloved within His bridal chamber, experienced through the Holy Spirit. Responsibility is about functioning effectively in our Kingdom duties through angelic interaction. Responsibility without intimacy is slavery. We cannot effectively govern as sons without intimacy.

Fruits, Gifts, and Angels

The *fruits* of the Spirit, the *gifts* of the Spirit, and the *angels of the Lord* are strongly entwined. If we look closely, we will notice that these different streams of Holy Spirit have a numerical value of *nine*. For instance, we have *nine gifts* of the Spirit, *nine order* of angels, and *nine fruits* of the spirit, all divided into three categories. I believe that the numerical value of nine represents the full expression and completeness of the work of the Holy Spirit.

As aforementioned, there are three aspects of the manifestation and operation of the person of the Holy Spirit of which I am currently aware: firstly, the *ministry of angels*; secondly, the operation of the *gifts* of the Spirit; thirdly, the *fruits* of the Spirit. Within the ministry of angels, according to the writings of Dionysius the Areopagite, Thomas Aquinas, and what we can find in the scriptures, there are nine main families of angels divided into three spheres:

"Above it stood the Seraphims: each one had six wings; with twain he covered his face, and with twain he covered his feet, and with twain he did fly." (Isaiah 6:2)

"Each of the four Cherubim had four faces: the first was the face of an ox, the second was a human face, the third was the face of a lion, and the fourth was the face of an eagle." (Ezekiel 10:14, NLT)

"And before the throne there was a sea of glass like unto crystal: and in the midst of the throne, and round about the throne, were four living creatures (zoes) full of eyes before and behind." (Revelation 4:7)

"Far above all principality, and power, and might, and dominion, and every name that is named, not only in this world, but also in that which is to come." (Ephesians 1:21)

"For by him were all things created, that are in heaven, and that are in earth, visible and invisible, whether they be thrones, or dominions, or principalities, or powers: all things were created by him, and for him." (Colossians 1:16)

1. The angelic canopy, which is the manifestation of the servitude aspect of the Son, through personified light beings.

Nine Orders and Families of Angels

1st Sphere Kingship	2nd Sphere Lordship	3rd Sphere Priesthood
Seraphim	Dominions/Lordships	Principalities/Rulership
Cherubim	Virtues/Strongholds	Archangels
Thrones (Zoes)	Powers/Authorities	Angels

2. The ministry of the gifts of the Holy Spirit, which has to do with man networking and interacting with angels, energized by the Spirit.

Nine Gifts of the Holy Spirit

Revelatory Gifts	Vocal Gifts	Power Gifts
Word of knowledge	Tongues	Gifts of healing
Word of wisdom	Interpretation of tongues	Working of miracles
Discernment of spirits	Prophecy	Faith

3. The fruits of the Spirit, which is the Holy Spirit releasing His breath into us. All in all, it is the Holy Spirit behind the scenes.

Nine Fruits of the Spirit

Love	Long suffering	Faithfulness
Joy	Kindness	Gentleness
Peace	Goodness	Self-control

The Three Spheres of Angels and the Three Divisions of Gifts

The angelic ministry has to do with angelic beings working out the protocols and desires of the Holy Spirit. I believe that the first sphere has to do with Kingship, the second sphere is Lordship, and the third has to do with Priesthood.

When we talk about the gifts of the spirit, they have mostly been equated with ministering to humanity. As we have classified the nine gifts of the spirit into three categories (revelatory, vocal, and power gifts), I want us to view each category as if it is linked to a part of the heavens: the first heavens, second heavens, and the third heavens.

In the context of the first heavens, I want us to zero in on the throne room. The throne room is the seat of YHVH wherein the first choir of angels is mostly found. I believe this realm of heaven is synonymous with the *revelatory gifts*. We can only see this link between the first choir of angels and the revelatory gifts if we approach these gifts not just in the usual way of ministering to people, but also ministering to YHVH. Let me explain.

A word of knowledge is a divine instantaneous knowing of someone, something, or an event. It is the revealing of hidden details of an individual. If you are having a word of knowledge concerning someone, you are receiving divine information about that individual which you did not know before. Now imagine having the same for YHVH, but instead of giving Him a word of knowledge, you are receiving divine revelation of His person. This is the hidden knowledge, the mysteries of Himself, being instantaneously downloaded to you without any form of learning or grid. Awesome, right? But how is this linked to the angels in the first choir?

If we notice in the first choir of angels--which I have said is linked to kingship due to the fact that the angels comprising this choir surround the crowned Lamb on His throne, and that it is the Revelation of the Son that makes one a king--these particular angels have distinct features. They all have more than two pairs of wings: the seraphim have six, the cherubim have four, and the zoes have six. But the distinct feature I want to talk about is their eyes. They are full of eyes, with the exception of the seraphim, who cover their faces.

The many eyes are there to capture and retain the divine knowledge of the beauty of YHVH. One set of insight (eyes) into YHVH is not enough to behold Him and know Him. The seraphim flying above the throne dwell in a perpetual state of awe and astonishment at His glorious beauty and knowledge. As they behold and receive divine knowledges of YHVH, they are compelled to cover up their faces and eyes. I believe within this first choir of angels, we see a higher degree of the personification of the gift of word of knowledge.

Another that is part of the revelatory gifts is that of the *discernment of spirits*. We have mostly used this gift in the context of discerning deception and the dark side. To discern is to understand, perceive, and know the nature of something. Let us imagine ourselves within the throne room, asking Holy Spirit to awaken our gift of discernment. In doing so, we are asking to be able to understand, perceive, and know the natures of the different light spectrums of Christ proceeding from His throne, to comprehend and know His ways.

I believe without a doubt that if we did so, we would begin to develop eyes within and without, just as the cherubim and zoes possess. Their eyes are also for understanding and discerning the ways of YHVH. The seraphim, cherubim, and zoes/thrones are discernment personified! Pause and ask YHVH to let you discern the nature of His light that He is imparting to you through reading this book.

The last in this class of gifts is the *word of wisdom*. A word of wisdom is the divine knowing of future events. It is also the knowing of the revelations of YHVH that He will usher into the future. In our "everyday churches," it is what we have grown to call and accept as prophecy.

If you notice, the books where the first choirs of angels were described in detail were all prophetic books. Isaiah's theme was on the coming Emmanuel and King of the Jews, Ezekiel's theme was the portrayal of Jesus as the Son of man, and John revealed the triumphant Word and His Bride. These were all words of wisdom directly unveiling revelations of Jesus that would come. The prophets who ushered in these "words of wisdom" of the Son interacted with an angel from the first choir of angels. Isaiah's iniquity was purged by a burning coal from a seraphim's hands. Ezekiel saw visions of God, but his first description of the visions of God were the cherubim! John was called by a zoe to come and take a look at the contents of the seven sealed scrolls. The zoes, cherubim, and seraphim are also "word of wisdom" personified.

They are the collective personification of the revelatory gifts and so much more. The kingship part has to do with being recipients of the direct revelations of the crowned Lamb upon the throne.

Again, ask YHVH for a word of wisdom. I asked for one concerning Himself in my life, and He said, "I want to bring revelations of the King in Me to you, so that you can operate and function as a King." You can ask Him, too. Do it now!

Let us parallel the second heavens to the second choir of angels and to the *vocal gifts*. This choir of angels has to do with *lordship*. I believe one part of our being co-heirs with Christ is to operate as lords. A lord is usually a ruler of a small designated area. We are to subdue and rule over areas within our lives, souls, and spheres of influence that have not been given over to the King. This allows us to be lords; hence, Yeshua is glorified in and through us as the Lord of lords. He is our Lord, and we are lords, too.

Another aspect of being a lord is also in the area of enforcing the Kingdom. This requires swift ways of communicating Kingdom strategies and blueprints. The angels in this choir are dominions, might, and powers. They are all an expression of a divine virtue of "force."

"From the days of Yohannan The Baptizer until this hour the Kingdom of Heaven is led by force and the violent are seizing it." (Matthew 11:12, Aramaic Version)

Our warfare is through the word of God. It is the energizing that comes from interactions with the frequencies from Jesus, the vocalizing of YHVH. Therefore, communication is essential, but this communication is God communicating His Son to us, in the person of the Holy Spirit.

The communication aspect is also in our vocal interaction with angels; hence, the vocal gifts. Also, as we will see later on in this book, dominions in the second choir of angels operate as divine translators of YHVH instructions, so there is a need for the vocal gifts.

Tongues and interpretation of tongues has to do with clearer and deeper communications. Prophecy is the divine speaking forth of God that comforts, edifies, and exhorts. To prophesy is not necessarily to tell of future events, as that is the word of wisdom. To prophesy is to raise the soul into the harmonies of heaven by ushering in the NOW word of God. Raising our being into the stream of heaven's goodness has to do with receiving the impartations of God's virtues. This involves the family of angels called virtues. Just as in the first choir of angels, the angels in this second choir are also vocal gifts personified and more.

Finally, we come to the third class of gifts, which are the power gifts. The power gifts have to do with the supernatural taking preeminence over this natural world. I have equated them with this earthly cosmos, that being the dimensions of the earth, its heavens, and even the astral heavens that we lost touch with when Adam fell. I have done this because in the realms of YHVH, there is not really a need for miracles, as miracles are the normalcy in that dimension. A miracle is considered a miracle in this realm because it is beyond and contrary to our physical properties. I have linked this class of gifts to the last choir of angels, which constitutes principalities, archangels, and angels. These angels are involved within the realm and affairs of the earthly cosmos.

It is highly improbable to see an angel from the first and second choirs working healings and miracles in church meetings. They are not designed for this atmosphere. The angels that we usually witness and interact with in healings and so forth are from this last choir of angels. To interact with the other angels, we have to live in an ascended state, which is the state of sonship. Sonship is the lifestyle of sitting and resting within the bosom of the ultimate Son Jesus.

Sonship as YHVH intends is a full fractal, three hundred and sixty degree spectrum of interacting with the angels from all three spheres. Thus, the trans-dimensional, ever-expanding spirit of men has to fully embrace and operate from the high energy light spectrums that are released in every sphere. The whole operation of the angelic canopy is the revealing of a matured son of God.

As we grow to maturity, angels of varying levels of authority will be assigned to us. It is difficult to say which ones, as we are likely to run the danger of trying to box in the expansive workings of these heavenly beings.

So, in a nutshell, angels of the Lord are spirit beings who enforce heaven's protocols and principles. They work alongside sons of YHVH in bringing the government of heaven to the full redemption of creation and the flooding of the glorious light of Yeshua into this cosmos.*

The *gifts of the Holy Spirit* are the glimpses into the function and operation of the domain of heaven's citizens in this earthly cosmos.

The *fruits of the Spirit* are the atmosphere and aura of heaven breaking into our souls. Angels carry auras of the fruits of the Spirit. Fruits come as a result of spending time in the realms of YHVH, which is also the manifested presence of Jesus.

I believe that when these three are evidenced in our lives -- constant interaction with the angelic choirs, operation of the gifts, and the manifestation of the fruits of the spirit -- we are operating in the fullness of a mature son.

Chapter 11

Living from Mount Zion

'*But ye are come unto mount Sion, and unto the city of the living God, the heavenly Jerusalem, and to an innumerable company of angels, to the general assembly and church of the firstborn, which are written in heaven, and to God the Judge of all, and to the spirits of just men made perfect, And to Jesus the mediator of the new covenant, and to the blood of sprinkling, that speaks better things than that of Abel." (Hebrews 12:22-24)*

In recent years, this scripture has been most profound for me personally. I particularly note the phrase *"an innumerable company of angels."* A short while ago, the church's understanding of the spiritual realities of heaven and angels was projected to a futuristic day when death would whisk us into heaven. Over the last few years, through God's gracious mercy, He has illuminated our minds to understand that the blood of Jesus has given us access into Mount Zion and, therefore, we do not have to wait for a futuristic encounter with the angels or heaven.

The psalmist David said,

"Out of Zion, the perfection of beauty, God hath shined." (Psalms 50:2)

He chose his words, as a man writing not from hearsay, but from seeing that great and majestic city and its affairs. He clearly saw God's position in Zion. To the psalmist, whose eyes had been granted the opportunity to see, he witnessed God coming *"out"* of Zion, and he observed that God's abode is *"in"* His Mountain. His dwelling place is in Mount Zion, and from within Zion, He comes out, resplendent in His beauty. How we are to perfectly reflect this! It is God on the inside of us, shining forth His beauty.

It is the beauty of the presence of God within us that attracts, allows, and establishes an ongoing relationship with angels. When the Kingdom is activated within us, the resplendent beauty of God is displayed through us.

When Jesus spoke to Thomas about the revelation of the Father, He said, "I am in the Father and the Father is in me." He further said, "The Kingdom of God is within you and the Kingdom of Heaven is at hand." The Lord in us brings heaven to earth, and us being in Him allows us to engage in the conscious realities of heaven. Hence, since we are the dwelling place of God, we are able to bring heaven to earth. We are a direct expression of the heavenly Mount Zion on this earth. Jesus said,

"You are the light of the world. You cannot hide a city that has been built upon a mountain." (Matthew 5:14, Aramaic Version)

We are God's living stones, with Jesus being the chief cornerstone, built upon a mountain. We are also the mountain, the government of YHVH established in this cosmos so that the beauty of the heavenly Mount Zion might be translated and made evident in this realm. The angels desire to behold God shining forth from within our spirit man. Let us not cage Him!

I want to give specific mention to *Hebrews 12:1:*

"Therefore, since we are surrounded by such a great cloud of witnesses..."

To see the glorious realities of heaven be made manifest on the earth would require us being surrounded by the angelic canopy. To be surrounded by the angelic canopy means we have to "surround" Yeshua. We are surrounded by such a great cloud of witness so that we in turn would surround Him. Again, I say, Jesus is the attraction of all of heaven. *To surround Him is to consciously focus our* thoughts, our emotions, our minds upon the Lord Jesus Christ, thus our entire lives are totally wrapped around Yeshua in a daily, experiential fellowship with Him. This is the art of mirroring the heavenly Mount Zion, *surrounded to surround Him,* by turning the gaze of the soul inwards, until all the outward distractions melt away and all are drawn to the beauty of the King Who is within.

As we learn to let His beauty emanate from within us, we, the City of God, begin to mirror the heavenly Mount Zion and a convergence and connection point is established, and the angelic canopy is activated to see His Kingdom come and His will be done on earth as it is in heaven. This is the twofold manifestation of His will being made manifest on earth as it is in heaven.

It is imperative that we jealously surround Him so that the realities of Zion will be realized in this cosmos with the help of the angelic canopy.

Jesus Shifted the Cosmic Consciousness

By virtue of the Son of God entering this cosmos, He completely changed and shifted the views of angels upon humanity. The fact that He took our very form has forever given great value and honor upon us from the angelic beings.

The fullness of the manifestation of the angelic canopy came into effect when the only begotten Son was manifested. His entrance into the universes brought with Him a widespread ministry of angels.

"And again, when he bringeth in the first begotten into the world, he saith, And let all the angels of God worship him." (Hebrews 1:6)

This "bringing forth" shows that when the omnipresent, omnipotent, omniscient God fully expressed Himself to all creation in YESHUA, He gave purpose and identity to all things. Through the revelation of the Father in Jesus Christ, angels found and realized that their purpose is to worship Him. Worship transcends singing and dancing. The angels' service to the Son is also an act of worship. So when the Son came into the universe, the angels became fully conscious of their purpose and their mandate.

Jesus Christ came into this cosmos as Light incarnate.The fall of Adam had darkened the minds of mankind. The entry of Jesus Christ enlightened humanity's mindsets, elevating us from our primitive state into a much more evolved one. All creation knowingly or unknowingly responded to the voice and frequencies of the Living Word. Creation's perception was elevated into the realms of the goodness of God, consciously, unconsciously, and sub-consciously. This increase in creation's consciousness means that higher and more positive frequencies are released from us.

Strong, high, and positive frequencies frame up a conducive atmosphere and territory that is essential for angels to work. Certain angelic beings need a particular platform to interact with us. Thus, we need to be flooded with the light of Christ, the light that is able to physically change the genetic makeup of our brain cells so that we can use our brains to its full capacity.

A mind that is illuminated with understanding, knowledge, and wisdom creates the platform that is essential for angels to open a deeper dimension of knowledge that one carries. For instance, Daniel understood the times and seasons of the Jews after studying the book of Jeremiah. Daniel desired to know, and out of desire, coupled with prayer and fasting, acquired knowledge, which resulted in an angelic visitation from Gabriel. Gabriel said to Daniel,

"I have come to give you skill and understanding." (Daniel 9:22)

Every good and perfect gift comes from above, so all forms of technological advancement and inventions are as a result of angelic assistance. This assistance is the result of Jesus Christ shifting the cosmic consciousness. Through the illumination of the light of Christ, mankind has, to a degree, formed a platform conducive enough for angelic interaction.

"That was the true Light, which lighteth every man that cometh into the world" (John 1:9)

The manifestation of the mind of Christ is the influx of heaven's light. Without Him expressing His mind, there are no Kingdom realities. Kingdom realities involve angelic activities, for His mind has knitted together an ongoing relationship with angels. The mind of Christ is the territory and realm in which angels flow.

Seated in Heavenly Places -- Spiritual Governmental Position

"And he (Legion) besought him much that he would not send them away out of the region." (Mark 5:10)

We need to understand that one of the most important things in the spiritual world is that of our governmental position, territories, and regions. There are particular Kingdom realities and angelic manifestations that will not take place until we rise to a particular domain. For instance, the main objective in Lucifer's heart was to rise to sit in a domain of sonship. This is evidenced in his remark in Isaiah 14:13-14, "*I will ascend above the stars and I will be like the most High God.*" Who else is like the most High God, except sons of the most High God?

Our identity of sonship is found in YHVH, and it is also a realm of governing and co-ruling with YHVH. There is a literal place of governance in Yeshua called "sonship."

One day, I meditated on the scriptures about how the enemy wanted to ascend to be like the Most High. As I mused over this, I saw a place in the spirit which I call "the domain of sonship." It was a vast realm of governmental authority, and in this place were many thrones. I saw that when a son sat upon the throne, he became one with the life of the throne. This place pulsates with the very life of YHVH in a higher degree than other realms. I understood that to fully function as a son, I had to be in that place. This is the realm that Satan wanted to ascend above, for only those who function and sit in this place of authority are truly like God.

Our Adamic soul prevents us from being aware that Yeshua has placed us in heavenly places in Him. We continuously need to ascend into Yeshua and contend for our place and position of authority. This ever ascension into Him should not just be a mental conception, but the reality of our simultaneous dwelling has to be experienced. And as we ascend, the shackles of the physical dimension that tethers us are broken.

Our thrones of authority in these heavenly places is the cherubim. Just as YHVH rides the cherub, the cherubim are to be our vehicle of expression of Kingdom realities in this metacosm (Psalms 18:10).

The cherubim are our seat of rest and governance. Sitting in these places of authority allows us to be perpetually energized by the currents of God's glory imparted through these high angelic beings. This allows us to release stronger frequencies. Stronger frequencies mean higher angelic authority.

Paul says, "heavenly places" (Ephesians 2:6). Have you ever wondered why it's not "place" but "places"? It is because our spirit man is capable of being multi-located when we enter in the cherubic seat. Look at how this ties perfectly with the cherubim. Ezekiel says,

"The beings could move in any of the four directions they faced, without turning as they moved." (Ezekiel 1:17, NLT)

A cherub has the ability to move to the four corners simultaneously. Therefore, riding upon the cherubim enables us, as sons, the function of being multi-located in I Am. Sitting on the cherubim energizes our spirit man to the capacity that we are able to project or be multi-present just as a cherub does when it projects itself to all the cardinal points. This allows for the expansion of our spirit man, thus increasing our spheres of authority. The expansion of my spirit man is like a king who is expanding his kingdom. A larger kingdom means more territory; more territory requires the employ of more generals, and in our case, the employment of more angels.

Christ Jesus Has Elevated Us

About three years ago, I read a verse in the book of Hebrews that triggered me on this journey of understanding the role of angels in the Old Testament. I began to see and understand that the law was given by Moses under the word spoken by angels. These angels who were used in the ordination of the law are a high class of beings. The dispensation of the law by angels signified an era of servanthood.

"...Who have received the law by the disposition of angels, and have not kept it." (Acts 7:53)

To fully comprehend and appreciate what Christ has done for us, we need to know our position with the angelic canopy prior to His death and resurrection.

The whole dispensation of the Mosaic order had to do with fallen man submitting under the sovereignty of the Lord through high angelic beings working as intermediaries. These beings were also referred to as elemental spirits, but not in terms of hierarchy. Thus, they are not base elementary beings.

Their mandate was to keep us under the elemental realms of this cosmos. That is why Jesus said, "No man has ascended to heaven except the Son of man who is in heaven" (John 3:13).

Ascending to heaven has to do with rising above the earthly metacosm, which is a combination of elemental properties and frequencies. The earthly metacosm was overseen by these "elemental spirits." The reason that no one was able to ascend into heaven prior to Christ was because our spiritual makeup vibrated at the same frequency of the earthly metacosm and we were tied to its frequency. John the Baptist and Paul said,

"He that cometh from above is above all: he that is of the earth is earthly, and speaketh of the earth: he that cometh from heaven is above all." (John 3:31)

"The first man is of the earth, earthy: the second man is the Lord from heaven. As is the earthy, such are they also that are earthy: and as is the heavenly, such are they also that are heavenly. And as we have borne the image of the earthy, we shall also bear the image of the heavenly." (1 Corinthians 15:47-49)

These elemental spirits or principalities and powers were the ceiling to the spiritual maturity of Israel. Let us now examine how all this incorporates the Mosaic dispensation.

"Wherefore then serveth the law? It was added because of transgressions, till the seed should come to whom the promise was made; and it was ordained by angels in the hand of a mediator." (Galatians 3:19)

One thing that Paul the apostle faced and tried to birth within the consciousness of his generation was the supremacy of Christ. The people in that era compared the message of Christ with the law. This comparison questioned the supremacy of Christ over the angelic beings that ordained (Galatians 3:19) and worked as intermediaries of the law. We can clearly see in Galatians 1 that Paul was not trying to validate the gospel, rather he was establishing the supremacy of the Christ when he said,

"But though we, or an angel from heaven, preach any other gospel unto you than that which we have preached unto you, let him be accursed." (Galatians 1:8)

These high angelic beings have been involved in the ordination and disposition of the Law of Moses. It was not that the angels whom Moses and all of Israel submitted to were opting to be served, but embedded within the consciousness of the people was the reality of the Old Covenant's way of engaging with God. This consciousness was a way of approaching YHVH from a servant and slave mentality, which put men under the word spoken by angels.

It seems to me that whenever Paul wrote about the Law of Moses, he equated it with *elemental spirits of the universe*, which he also calls powers and principalities.

"See to it that no one makes a prey of you by philosophy and empty deceit, according to human tradition, according to the elemental spirits of the universe and not according to Christ." (Colossians 2:8, Revised Standard Version)

"If with Christ you died to the elemental spirits of the universe, why do you live as if you still belonged to the world? Why do you submit to regulations, 'Do not handle, Do not taste, Do not touch' (referring to things which all perish as they are used), according to human precepts and doctrines? These have indeed an appearance of wisdom in promoting rigour of devotion and self-abasement and severity to the body, but they are of no value in checking the indulgence of the flesh." (Colossians 2:20, RSV)

*"I mean that the heir, as long as he is a child, is no better than a slave, though he is the owner of all the estate; but he is under **guardians and trustees** until the date set by the father. So with us; when we were children, we were slaves to the **elemental spirits of the universe**. But when the time had fully come, God sent forth his Son, born of woman, born under the law, to redeem those who were under the law, so that we might receive adoption as sons. And because you are sons, God has sent the Spirit of his Son into our hearts, crying, 'Abba! Father!' So through God you are no longer a slave but a son, and if a son then an heir." (Galatians 4:1-7 RSV)*

"Wherefore then serveth the law? It was added because of transgressions, till the seed should come to whom the promise was made; and it was ordained by angels in the hand of a mediator." (Galatians 3:19)

"For if the word spoken by angels was steadfast, and every transgression and disobedience received a just recompense of reward." (Hebrews 2:2)

In the Mosaic dispensation, there was no real co-relation of mankind with sonship. The revealing of the Father, which is the message of Jesus, is paramount to us being revealed as sons. This is because the coming of Jesus into the hearts *of those who are reborn* has placed us into a positional union with Him wherein we are no longer servants but sons, as Yeshua is. Sons have been entrusted to sit in the bosom of the ultimate Son Yeshua, thus rising above the elemental spirits of the universe.

We are seated in Christ above principalities and powers. These principalities and powers are both the fallen ones and the ones which helped in the establishment of the law. Prior to the triumph of Christ on the cross, mankind was under the domain and rule of these principalities and powers.

The whole era of grace is the elevation of Adam above these angels; thus, that which man was under now becomes subjected to him in Christ Jesus.

The scriptures say that we will judge the angels, but they are not subject to us as though we are their lord and master. They are only subject in relation to obedience to the Word of the Lord of Hosts, Jesus Christ. The magnificent awe of the angels toward us is this amazing, divine transfer of how man, who was at first made a little lower than angels, has now been made higher than the angels.

"You made him lower than the angels for a short time; You crowned him with glory and honour." (Hebrews 2:7, HCS)

The phrase "a little lower" implies how man was subject to the angels. This glorious trade has made angels desire to comprehend the mysteries of Christ through our lives. We are to them a played out orchestra of the Love of the Father. Encoded within our spirit man is the beauty and blueprint of heaven, so angels desire to gaze into this beauty emanating from us through our ongoing ascension into Jesus Christ. This allows them to work as divine translators of heaven's glory in this cosmos.

Let us look at what Paul says the purpose of the Church is.

"His intent was that now, through the church, the manifold wisdom of God should be made known to the rulers and authorities in the heavenly realms, according to his eternal purpose that he accomplished in Christ Jesus our Lord." (Ephesians 3:10)

"God's purpose in all this was to use the church to display his wisdom in its rich variety to all the unseen rulers and authorities in the heavenly places." (Ephesians 3:10, NLT)

"To the intent that now unto the principalities and powers in heavenly places might be known by the church the manifold wisdom of God." (Ephesians 3:10, KJV)

"That by the church would be made known the full-diverse wisdom of God to Principalities and to Rulers who are in Heaven." (Ephesians 3:10, Aramaic Bible)

"The purpose of this enlightenment is that through the church the multifaceted wisdom of God should now be disclosed to the rulers and the authorities in the heavenly realms." (Ephesians 3:10, NET Bible)

We will further delve into elemental spirits in depth, so continue with me on this amazing journey.

Translators of Heaven - Communication

One of the mandates of angels is to bring the glorious dimensions of heaven into this realm. They work as divine translators of heavenly realities, so encoded within their makeup is the beauty of heaven. All of their acts with humanity are to raise our consciousness and emotions into the harmonies of heaven.

The gestures of the angels are the symphonic harmonies of the love of the Father. God sings over His beloved and this love song of the Father is well embedded into the spiritual makeup of angels. They are personified music. It is written of Lucifer,

"The workmanship of your tabrets and of your pipes was prepared in you in the day that you were created." (Ezekiel 28:13)

It was not only Lucifer who was made like this. All angels, to some degree, were created in this fashion. They bring heaven with them. Their ministry is vast, blissful, and so magnificent that one might be inclined to worship them. They are made from the light of the chief luminary, Jesus Christ, Who is the very source of all creation.

There is a ceaseless communication of God to creation, and oftentimes the word of God to us is translated in the persona of our angel, his character, or his spiritual makeup. Many of us have met the same angels in our journeys in the Lord. The spiritual makeup of certain types of angels is influenced and changed according to the word of God that they bring to us. Some of our personal angels morph into the image of the word spoken by YHVH. Some of them have characteristics that we have not yet come across as humans. These characteristics all originate from the glory of God, thus angels are translators of Christ's glorious manifestations. Being translators of YHVH's glory means they usher in a glory of Jesus specifically formulated to be released and ministered to us by them.

Angelic Communication

To open the realms of angelic manifestation, we need to live a life consciously aware of the spiritual dimensions. The doorway to these manifestations is the presence of Jesus. I have found worship to be the key.

I remember one day in worship, I became aware that I had some heavenly visitors. There were four angels standing in my room in a semi-circle. One was behind the other three and looked very jovial. He was bald with a strong muscular build, but had the playfulness of a child. He wore no shirt, but had on a garment that crisscrossed his chest like an "X," and he carried two swords. His bulky build and swords were a dead giveaway that he was a warring angel. I thought to myself, "I have never seen a warring angel with this giddy childlike quality." Each time I looked at him, I burst into laughter and he would rock excitedly. I had expected a much more vigorous and robust demeanor from a warring angel.

The angel standing at the beginning of the semi-circle communicated to me that the Lord was giving me covering in this season of my life. This communication was not verbal, but was clear by the way he manifested himself. When I looked at him, this angel expanded his wings and covered me. The angel in the middle brought a message to me that God was establishing me in a firm foundation. He translated this by planting his staff firmly into the ground with a powerful authority. The other angel was serious, simple, and quiet, but communicated his name, which was his assignment.

After this encounter, I entered a difficult season in my life, where everything I was standing on as my security was shaken. I realized that if the Lord was firmly planting me in His foundation, it meant that everything I had established would be shaken. There were certain things that I had established that I lost in that season. If I had remembered this encounter earlier, I might have responded to my circumstances in a much more positive and optimistic way. The joyful warring angel was "the joy of the Lord is my strength" as he battled on my behalf. The covering angel covered me in a time of shaking. The staff planting angel made sure that only what the Lord had established would stand and that my faith would be rooted in the foundation of YHVH.

God always precedes our difficult moments with the necessary graces to help us through. There is so much grace for every difficult situation. YHVH has already finished the work and we are to work with the angels to enforce it, but what is required is a hopeful heart to trigger the results.

Another example of angelic heart-to-heart communication was when I was invited to a friend's church. We were worshiping and suddenly an angel appeared in the front of the congregation. He was formed as if a whirlwind of light energy had been compressed to create his body. He did not smile or speak to me, but as I looked at him, I knew who he was. He was Winds of Change. Then I heard him say, "Winds of change, I bring winds of change." I knew he was not a personal angel to me, but that his assignment was to bring winds of change to this gathering.

Three months later, I did a follow up, and my friend told me that everything had changed and shifted. Our Heavenly Father is constantly speaking and the angels bring His messages to us. We have to be conscious of the Kingdom realms of our Father.

Some time ago, I was preaching in a small town in Ontario. My notes were jumbled and this made it difficult for me to fully convey my message. I remembered that I was talking about Jesus being the perfection of God's goodness, yet, when the rich young ruler addressed Jesus as "good Master," Jesus said to him, "There is none good but God." This seemed to contradict what I was saying about the goodness of Jesus. From the scriptures, he seemed to reject being called good by this young rich ruler. Immediately the angel who was on my right spoke to me and I understood why the Lord had responded that way. The ruler was addressing Jesus on the *base earthly* level that he saw Jesus. To him, Jesus was just an earthly, morally good man, and Jesus answered him on the level of his perception of Jesus. It was the principal of receiving a prophet in a prophet's name. He saw Jesus as a normal good man, and as a normal man, Jesus spoke to him. I did not see the angel, but I knew it was not the Holy Spirit as I have come to understand that the communication of the angelic is not internal, but it is external.

This communication is beyond any earthly one. It is as if the words are spoken outside of time, so they do not need a time processing factor for our brains to understand them. I would call it an instantaneous download of messages which bypasses time. Words have become a realm that I can see into, freeing from my brain trying to process the information.

Chapter 12

The Presence of YHVH and His Angels

*"H*is *Voice is His Presence, His Presence is the climax, the pinnacle of all spiritual experiences. He is constantly speaking; speaking His Person out.*

Angels, they bring messages, and often times their message is not verbally given, it is translated through their actions.

It had been a rough week, and I needed some word of encouragement or an impartation of strength. I was going through my everyday work routine, musing upon the Lord but feeling dejected. I wanted the Lord to speak to me, and I wanted to feel the canopy of His embrace, but I had forgotten that He speaks through the gestures and the body language of His angels. While I was putting a pile of heavy objects on top of a shelf, skinny, lanky me was staggering and struggling when a huge angel appeared. His skin tone was cream-ish with a slight golden hue, and a beautiful euphoria exuded from him. The angel jokingly taunted me by flexing his muscles, in a rather comical, childish way. It was more like, "Hey, Michael! I can move that with one finger. Maybe you could use me." I laughed heartily, realizing through the angel's "comedic body language" that we often carry the burdens of life that Yeshua has already bore.

The universal corporate function of angels is as messengers. A messenger carries a message, either a verbal, written, or a recorded communication. God's message has always been Jesus Christ. YHVH is not trying to communicate letters on a page or some motivational speech. He has been and is always communicating His Son to the entire cosmos translated as His presence with us.

When YHVH speaks, He speaks Himself to an individual. He imparts Himself to the individual with whom He is communicating. He Himself, the Living Word, imparts His essence to an angel and becomes the message the angel brings. The Lord can send an angel with a message, expressed as the Presence of God manifested in our midst. Often times, what we think is the presence of God is basically angels communicating forth the word of YHVH.

His voice can be expressed as His tender presence taking its rest and abode in us. Sometimes, it is a sensation, an expression of laughter, a healing, a sign, a wonder, a tingling, or just the "comedic body language" of your angel. All this accumulates and points to the supreme message of YHVH, which is His Son Jesus Christ.

Angels carry depths and different degrees of the presence of the Lord, and the presence of the Lord they bring is the message they carry. Angels never come to communicate themselves. They come to communicate the voice that is proceeding from the mouth of YHVH, and that voice is Jesus Christ, imparting His presence in our midst.

"Are they not all ministering spirits, sent forth to minister to them who shall be heirs of salvation?" (Hebrews 1:14)

A genuine encounter with angels will always leave Jesus imprinted in our hearts, for their message is Jesus. His presence is imparted into our midst through a divine interaction with His hosts. He is Jehovah Sabaoth, Lord of the Angel Armies.

The Name above All Names

"Being made so much better than the angels, as he hath by inheritance obtained a more excellent name than they." (Hebrews 1:4)

The rank and authority of an angel is determined by the name the angel carries. When Gabriel told Mary his name, it wasn't merely, "I am Gabriel." The utterance of his name to Mary came with great frequencies of authority. Jesus has been given the name which is above all names (Philippians 2:9) and it is only in His name that we can truly instruct and send forth angels. One has authority and access to the angelic canopy to the degree that he stands in the name of Yeshua, but what does it mean to be in His name?

In Hebrew, a name usually denotes character and nature. The only way we can operate in true authority is from standing within His name, which is being immersed within His very nature and character.

Being in the name of Jesus is being in the realm of the manifestation of His presence. His presence is the unveiling of His essence.

When God created Adam, He breathed into him. The Hebrew word for breath is *neshammah*. The word *neshammah** means personality, character, nature, and essence. So the personality, character, and essence of YHVH is through the manifestation of His name. I believe YHVH literally whispered His name into Adam when He breathed into him. So being in His name is being surrounded by the frequencies of His personality, character, and essence. It is in this place that we can truly say we bear a name that is above all names.

The breath of YHVH proceeding from us is the manifestation of the reality of standing in His name. When we engage with angels, it should be from standing within the abiding and authority of His name. This safeguards us from interacting with fallen angels.

The name that He has received is not only the name of Jesus, but also the way the Father refers to Him as His Beloved Son. Through Christ Jesus, many sons have been brought forth to glory, and because He addresses us as sons, we too have been made so much better than the angels, as we have inherited a much more excellent name than they. But remember, the name is an inheritance, and only through one's dying can one obtain that name. No person alive to self can be called a son of God. Jesus Christ, the ultimate Son, was (once) made a little lower than the angels for the suffering of death, and through this death, He was lifted up to God, crowned with glory and honor.

The path has not changed. Angelic hosts are awaiting the instructions of the sons. Sons are those who have so humbled themselves through much suffering of death that through dying to self, they are crowned with glory and honor. It's that crown of glory and honor that angels revere and honor when they look at us. The crown is obtained by following His path, a path marked by bleeding feet and wet with many tears. So let us not be afraid to place our hands in His nailed-scarred palms. He is able to bear us where we cannot bear ourselves.

The scriptures say that unless we suffer with Him, we cannot reign with Him. To rule and reign with Him is to manifest His glory on the earth. Entering into the fellowship of His suffering brings us into union with Christ. He learned obedience through the things He suffered, and we also will learn obedience; thus, His glory will be made manifest as we enter into the realm of the name that is above every other name.

He has been glorified, seated above principalities and rulers in heavenly places. This is the place of our authority. This is the place where we are also seated in Him, and it is from this place that we are able to function in our authority to command the angels. Let us not go around instructing angels if we have not yet entered into the fellowship of His sufferings.

Chapter 13

The Vortex of YHVH

*"*T*hen said he unto me, Prophesy unto the wind, prophesy, son of man, and say to the wind, Thus saith the Lord GOD; Come from the four winds, O breath, and breathe upon these slain, that they may live." (Ezekiel 37:9)*

The paper was gently laid on the table. In the center of that one sheet of paper was a whirlwind. It was a living two-dimensional drawing of a whirlwind. It was a mixture of various violent currents of winds exuding an indigo-pinkish color. I zeroed in with childlike curiosity. I observed that the vortex of the winds was in the center of the four cardinal points.

On each cardinal point appeared wings. I instantly understood that they represented the angelic hierarchy, i.e the three different choirs of angels. The whirlwind parted into four winds, with each wind settling upon each angel's wings. The north and south winds, east and west winds, embedded themselves respectively within the spiritual makeup of the angels. God was in the winds encompassing the ministry of His four winds, encoding every spiritual impulse, gesture, and flow of the angels by His breath. "YHVH rides on the wings of the winds" (Psalms 18:10).

This encounter or "vision in the night" was a key for me to understand how He makes His angels "winds": through the convergence of angelic beings with the winds of God.

"His way is in the whirlwind and the storm, and clouds are the dust of his feet." (Nahum 1:3 NIV)

The winds of YHVH are some of the most unusual expressions of the Holy Spirit that have been assigned to this cosmos. They allow His love and mercy to frame mankind by releasing winds of change. Each one of these winds is layered in every dimension of creation and each one is a doorway of change. This change is about one thing: being changed into the image and likeness of YHVH. These winds of change are known as the east, west, north, and south winds. We will notice these four seasons operating in our personal lives and the body of Christ as a whole. If we surrender to the vortex of YHVH, we will have access to the fullness and the workings of the Lord's Spirit in our lives.

I believe that the four cardinal winds are assigned to this cosmos for four seasons: judgment, deliverance, restoration, and transition. According to the fourth Hebrew letter, *Dalet,* the number four is an open door. So within the release of the four winds of YHVH and its very vortex is Jesus Christ, Who *is* the Door or Vortex of the WINDS OF CHANGE in its entirety. Jesus stood within the vortex of the four winds, encapsulated within the whirlwind of YHVH. The Son of man operated from within this place; thus, He knew the networking of the angels that ushered in the winds of God. He had a relationship with the operation of angels, who usher the winds of YHVH. You, too, can have this relationship with the angels!

The strength in heaven's relationships lies within the intimate exchange of the love of Christ and the deep consciousness of that love that in all things He has preeminence. The Holy Spirit manifests Himself in the likeness of the winds of YHVH, and because of the strong family relationship that exists between Himself and the angels, He makes his angels winds. The "making" as outlined in Psalms 104:4 is the deep entwining and the morphing of the angels' spiritual makeup with YHVH's vortex. This allows the angel to become an usher of the Winds of God. Some of us have even experienced these winds supernaturally when we have felt a breeze blow into a room without ventilation. But it's more than a breeze; it's also the changing of the seasons in our lives.

As we have established before, according to writings in angelology, we have nine orders of angels divided into three different spheres. The first sphere constitutes the seraphim, the cherubim, and thrones. The second sphere is comprised of dominions, virtues, and powers. The third sphere is composed of principalities, archangels, and angels. There is an order of seraphim that is solely responsible for bringing the north wind of God, and another seraphim order solely responsible of bringing the east wind of YHVH, and so on.

Let us look at principalities for further clarity. Principalities are warring angels over regions, territories, or land. One of their mandates is to usher in the Winds of YHVH over territories, regions, and lands and to oversee and protect their affairs. There are principalities who specifically work as ushers of the north winds, others are ushers of the south winds, and then others of the east and west winds. So, the branch of the family of principalities which exist just to bring in the north wind should be known as North Wind Principalities. We also have East Wind Principalities, South Wind Principalities, and West Wind Principalities. With that brief understanding of the corporate role of principalities, what is the role and the purpose of the north wind of YHVH?

*"Fair weather cometh out of the **north**: with God is terrible majesty." (Job 37:22)*

*"Great is the LORD, and greatly to be praised, In the city of our God, His holy mountain. Beautiful in elevation, the joy of the whole earth, Is Mount Zion in the far **north**, The city of the great King. God, in her palaces, Has made Himself known as a stronghold...." (Psalms 48:1-3)*

"For thou hast said in thine heart, I will ascend into heaven, I will exalt my throne above the stars of God: I will sit also upon the mount of the congregation, in the sides of the north." (Isaiah 14:13)

*"And I looked, and, behold, a whirlwind came out of the **north**, a great cloud, and a fire infolding itself, and a brightness was about it, and out of the midst thereof as the colour of amber, out of the midst of the fire." (Ezekiel 1:4)*

The north wind is the one that brings an ever-increasing revelation of the person of the Lord Jesus Christ, a deep, conscious, experiential unveiling of Himself which releases the awe of the Lord. The force of the north wind powers throughout the earth bringing the dominion, majesty government of YHVH. This is the place that the enemy coveted. Lucifer saw this as the place of sovereignty. Remember His throne is in the north (Isaiah 14:13, Ezekiel 1:4). This does not mean that YHVH is confined to one place, but rather, it concerns the governing of the cosmos. We know that heaven is His throne and earth His footstool.

There is a family of principalities whose chief assignment is to guard and defend the revelation of God that the North Wind brings over a nation. Their mandate is to guard against other wayward winds of false revelations of God. One may ask, "why is it we have a wide variety of false new age 'revelations' of God?" This is because the Lord unveils Himself to His children, born of His spirit, the true seekers of God.

The enemy is ushering a counterfeit north wind of himself to the masses. The principalities of the north winds of YHVH protect our ears from the influence of these false winds. Remember, if you ask Yeshua for bread, He will not give you a stone. As the north wind also brings in the manifestation of the governing seat of YHVH within us, these principalities make sure that the government of YHVH is established in a land, region, or territory through His sons.

The South Wind and the Angels

"Awake, O north wind; and come, thou south; blow upon my garden, that the spices thereof may flow out. Let my beloved come into his garden, and eat his pleasant fruits." (Songs 4:16)

"How thy garments are warm, when he quiets the earth by the south wind?" (Job 37:17)

The assignment of the angels to usher in the south winds speaks of the compassion of YHVH as He releases the warmth of the south winds. It invites creation to turn its face toward Him. It is a wind that brings provisions, refreshment, and rest.

*"Turn you to the stronghold, ye prisoners of hope: even to day do I declare that I will **restore** double unto thee; When I have bent Judah for me, filled the bow with Ephraim, and raised up thy sons, O Zion, against thy sons, O Greece, and made thee as the sword of a mighty man. And the LORD shall be seen over them, and his arrow shall go forth as the lightning: and the Lord GOD shall blow the trumpet, and shall go with **whirlwinds of the south**." (Zechariah 9: 12-14)*

Notice that He says He will restore you double. The restoration is manifested and brought about by the south wind. Restoration always releases rest, provisions, and refreshments. The avenue that the winds flow to creation is through the angels, thus, again, we have South

Wind Principalities, South Wind Dominions, South Wind Virtues, etc.

For further clarity with how angels are linked with the operation of the Winds of YHVH, let us look at dominions. Dominions are chief angels who relay YHVH's decisions and instructions to other angels. Dominions are in the second sphere, and I believe they work closely with the zoes (living creatures/thrones).

Like principalities or other angelic orders, the family of dominions are there specifically to release the encoded messages and instructions of YHVH's south winds to lesser angels. When I say "lesser," this does not by any means diminish the importance of their mandates and assignments.

Dominion angels are guardians of YHVH's blueprints. They have a wider spectrum of the counsels of God, as they stand in the Sode of YHVH. The "Sode of God" is the Council of the secrets and blueprints of God. It is concealed and intimate.

"Were you listening at God's secret council? Do you have a monopoly on wisdom?" (Job 15:8, NIV)

Herein YHVH's secrets are revealed, and these are not at all words of knowledge or what is coming in our way in the future. The secrets of the Lord are the intricate, hidden mysteries of YHVH that would bridge heaven and earth together in harmony. Since the dominions operate from within YHVH's Sode, they have a universal angelic language. This allows them to seamlessly communicate with other angels at a higher and clearer degree.

When we stand in the Council of YHVH and receive prophetic words or instructions, it is the dominion angels which make sure our guardian angels have clarity of God's instructions concerning us. They encode within other angels' spiritual makeup the destiny scrolls of the angels. Yes, angels have destiny scrolls.

In simple terms, I would say dominions operate as prophets to lesser angels. They function as elaborators, beings who perfectly articulate the mysteries and blueprints of YHVH. Making plain the workings of YHVH invites other angels to walk in experiential union with what YHVH is doing.

So we have dominion angels whose assignments are to bring an unfolding of the seasons and the purposes as to where, when, and how the winds are to blow. There are North Wind Dominions, South Wind Dominions, and a family of East Wind and West Wind Dominions.

The east wind, in a nutshell, is the wind of judgment that will blow before a new day (Exodus 14: 21). The west wind is the wind that brings deliverance (Exodus 10:19).

To summarize, the Lord of Hosts is encapsulated within the vortex of the four winds. He is the One who sits upon the circle of the earth and commands the release of the winds. The four winds will ever be coming around and around to suck us into the whirlwind of God's Love, who is Yeshua.

Chapter 14

The Mystery of His Name

"*Behold, I send an Angel before you, to keep you in the way, and to bring you into the place which I have prepared. Beware of him, and obey his voice, provoke him not; for he will not pardon your transgressions: for my name is in him." (Exodus 23:20-21)*

The redemptive names of YHVH have spirits (angels) that stand to manifest and serve according to the nature, character, and revelations of that particular name of YHVH. The Lord always assumes a name based on what aspect of His nature He wants to directly translate, impart, and reveal to creation. YHVH invites us into the exploration of the various wings of His household to which we belong, through us entering into His names.

In every name of YHVH, there is a family of spirits that operate under and from within the banner of that name. For instance, when YHVH reveals Himself as YHVH Rapha, He is inviting us to interact with and to know the family of spirits under that name's canopy. Raphael is a chief angel who belongs to this family of angels who manifest the service of YHVH Rapha.

Moses won the war against the Amalekites by lifting up his hands to the revelation of YHVH Nissi, The Lord My Banner. It was an act of surrender to the flow and will of the Holy Spirit as YHVH Nissi. Israel won this battle against the Amalekites because she received aid from the angels under the canopy of the name YHVH Nissi. This particular angelic ministry was triggered by the posture of Moses' body. Sometimes our body language is essential for angelic intervention.

We have angels that belong to the revelations of YHVH Shammah, YHVH Jireh, YHVH Raah, YHVH Tsidkenu, YHVH Shalom, and so on.

The seven spirits of the Lord before His throne also have angels that operate under them. These angels work as extensions of the seven spirits of the Lord.

"And the spirit of the LORD shall rest upon him, the spirit of wisdom and understanding, the spirit of counsel and might, the spirit of knowledge and of the fear of the LORD." (Isaiah 11:2)

We can see that there are the angels of the Lord, under the Spirit of the Lord. There are angels that belong to the branch of the spirit of wisdom; angels from the family of the spirit of understanding, the spirit of counsel, and the spirit of might; angels who are infused with and operate under the spirit of knowledge and the spirit of the fear of the Lord. These are some of the branches of the heavenly family of spirits.

The way these angelic beings interact and speak with us is often through manifesting the operations related to the seven spirits of God they stand beneath. For instance, the angel who belongs to the family of the spirit of wisdom and understanding will often speak to you through understanding. He gives you insight, comprehension, and deep perceptibility into situations, people's lives, and mysteries. You might have a divine comprehension of a person's personality, or of scriptures out of the blue, or of what is happening in a meeting, or what God is doing. There is a channel of angels speaking to you, through understanding and spiritual illumination.

Chapter 15

Elemental Spirits:
Ordainers of the Law

"*Y*ou received the Law as ordained by angels, and yet you haven't obeyed it!" *(Acts 7:53)*

"*Why then was the Law given? It was added because of transgressions, until the arrival of the seed to whom the promise referred. It was administered through angels by a mediator.*" *(Galatians 3:19)*

We touched a little on a class of beings referred to by Paul as *elemental spirits* of the universe. Let us try and understand their role in-depth. To fully know about the *elemental spirits* of the universe, we need to understand the reason angels were so prominent in the giving of the law. Most of what happened in the Old Testament had to do with the prophets interacting with angels (Hebrews 2:2). To a certain degree, YHVH was not directly involved, as His longing is to unveil Himself as a Father.

Jesus said that "they shall all be taught of God" (John 6:45). Yeshua was the beginning and the fulfilling of this prophecy. If you notice in John 6:45, Yeshua equates the interpersonal teaching of God with Fatherhood. The teaching of the Father brings us to the Son, and makes us partakers of the Son's nature. Through being with the Son, we enter into sonship.

Old Testament Israel never partook of Sonship because the involvement of angels in the ordination of the law had to do with the dispensation of the times. This was an era wherein the earth was void of sons of YHVH. There was no sonship, as sonship flows from the heart of the Father. These were times of servants, which was totally off from what YHVH had purposed. The message spoken in those times was ordained by angels. The message spoken by the angels was vastly different from the message spoken by the ultimate Son Jesus.

"*If the word spoken by angels was steadfast and every transgression and disobedience received a just recompense of reward; how shall we escape if we neglect so great a salvation; which at first began to be spoken by the Lord, and was confirmed unto us by them that heard him.*" *(Hebrews 2:3-4)*

The message of the Son is superior to that of angels, as it is the revelation of the Father. Let us look at the Father's message. From the beginning, God has always desired to reproduce after His kind. He wants sons who are molded and crafted in His heart and encapsulated within His Light. Sonship is the sermon and heartbeat of YHVH. Sonship is the perpetual revealing of our true identity which comes from standing under the glorious light of His Face. It is a life of an uninterrupted gaze upon the face of YHVH, for the image of the sons is found within the face of the Father. Thus, sonship begins with the revealing of the Father. We are consciously operational as sons of God to the degree that we know our Father, for to be a son is to be a recipient of the unceasing revelations of the Father.

The revelation of the Father can only rest upon those who have received the power to become the sons of God (John 1:12). Jesus is the ultimate Son, whose light alone carries sonship. Adam lived under this light, and by virtue of the fall, became estranged from Yeshua's light of sonship. This resulted in separation from his Father and a state of orphanhood, hence, Adam's unceasing revelation of the Father was cut short. The earth no longer had a functional son to reveal the Father and the Father no longer had a "manifest son" on the earth. Without the sons of God on the earth to bring forth the consciousness and dominion of YHVH, our earth was thrown into darkness.

YHVH created a good earth, and He desired a good earth, but only His consciousness can maintain the tide of His goodness. And since Adam could no longer bring "God consciousness," YHVH put forth the law as a "*school master,*" which aided in creation's harmony.

Although the law could not reveal the Father, it brought a certain level of YHVH's consciousness, but **not** from the eye of a son. Since it was ordained by high angelic beings, which Paul calls "*elemental spirits of the cosmos.*" It was a shadow of insight into how the Father is, but from a servant's perspective. It was a shadow, a silhouette, not the full picture! This shadow of YHVH allowed Israel to be the salt of the earth, as its perception and consciousness of YHVH brought harmony.

Let us look at the ordination of the law and its disposition to the great prophet Moses:

"He (Moses) was in the assembly in the wilderness, with the angel who spoke to him on Mount Sinai, and with our ancestors; and he received living words to pass on to us." (Acts 7:38, NIV)

"Then went up Moses, and Aaron, Nadab, and Abihu, and seventy of the elders of Israel: And they saw the God of Israel: and there was under his feet as it were a paved work of a sapphire stone, and as it were the body of heaven in his clearness." (Exodus 24:11)

It's such an interesting divine paradox between Stephen's sermon and what Moses recorded in Exodus. Stephen clearly distinctly illustrates that Moses spoke with "an angel" on Mount Sinai when he was with the elders. It seems this was common knowledge in Jewish tradition, as the Pharisees that Stephen was preaching to did not refute his statement.

When Moses recorded Exodus 24:11, he most likely wrote it as *"the Elohim of Israel."* The generic term *"Elohim,"* refers to the true God, as well as to *false gods, supernatural beings, high angelic beings, and angels.* The God of Israel (Angel of Israel) which the elders and Moses beheld was most likely the angel of the Lord assigned to Israel at that time. The words of Jesus validate this, our Lord said, "No man has seen God," since God can only be seen in the Son, as the Son alone can reveal the Father (John 1:18).

Many questions arise from this. Was it surely an angel or was it God on Mount Sinai? After all, on Mount Sinai, "God" almost destroyed all of Israel due to their rebellion. Surely an angel cannot do that, or can he?

"Who shall separate us from the love of Christ? shall tribulation, or distress, or persecution, or famine, or nakedness, or peril, or sword? As it is written, For thy sake we are killed all the day long; we are accounted as sheep for the slaughter. Nay, in all these things we are more than conquerors through him that loved us. For I am persuaded, that neither death, nor life, nor angels, nor principalities, nor powers, nor things present, nor things to come, Nor height, nor depth, nor any

other creature, shall be able to separate us from the love of God, which is in Christ Jesus our Lord." (Romans 8:35-39)

When Paul penned this famous verse, it was more than an allegory of the vastness of the love of God. As much as this sounds like a declaration and statement of faith on how great the love of God is, the apostle gives us insight into how, prior to Christ, creation could be separated from being partakers of the love of God.

I want us to understand that everything Paul mentioned in this verse had the ability to come between us and the love of God prior to Christ's death. For instance, the great Apostle mentions nakedness and the sword. Was it not nakedness that made Adam hide and separate himself from the God who is Love? And was it not a flaming sword that stood as a chasm between fallen man and Eden, thus separating mankind from the tree of life who is our Lord? If we go through the scriptures, we notice that everything Paul wrote down in that passage separated man from God in the Old Testament. With that being noted, I want to emphasize my point on *"angels, principalities, and powers."*

The high angelic beings that were instrumental in the ordination of the law had the capacity to come between the manifestation of God's love. The angel of the Lord that worked with Moses had the God-given authority to forgive sins. YHVH says this of him:

"Behold, I send an Angel before thee, to keep thee in the way, and to bring thee into the place which I have prepared. Beware of him, and obey his voice, provoke him not; for he will not pardon your transgressions: for my name is in him. But if thou shalt indeed obey his voice, and do all that I speak; then I will be an enemy unto thine enemies, and an adversary unto thine adversaries." (Exodus 23:20-22)

If we look closely through Exodus, we will see that the angel had the authority to be a barrier between mankind and God. Remember, in this era, humanity was under the ceiling and authority of YHVH through the elemental spirits of the universe.

An interesting dialogue happened between Moses and *Elohim* on Mount Sinai. In this incident, Moses, a mortal, managed to make *Elohim* repent of the just punishment that was supposed to be meted out to the people.

"And the LORD said unto Moses, I have seen this people, and, behold, it is a stiff necked people: Now therefore let me alone, that my wrath may wax hot against them, and that I may consume them: and I will make of thee a great nation. And Moses besought the LORD his God, and said, LORD, why doth thy wrath wax hot against thy people, which thou hast brought forth out of the land of Egypt with great power, and with a mighty hand? Wherefore should the Egyptians speak, and say, For mischief did he bring them out, to slay them in the mountains, and to consume them from the face of the earth? Turn from thy fierce wrath, and repent of this evil against thy people. Remember Abraham, Isaac, and Israel, thy servants, to whom thou swarest by thine own self, and saidst unto them, I will multiply your seed as the stars of heaven, and all this land that I have spoken of will I give unto your seed, and they shall inherit it for ever. And the LORD repented of the evil which he thought to do unto his people." (Exodus 32:9-14)

We know clearly from Stephen's sermon in Acts 7 that it was an angel of the Lord who was with Moses on Mount Sinai. Can we safely say that this angel who deputized for YHVH had been provoked by rebellious Israel (Exodus 23:20-22)? The angel had been provoked and sinned against; therefore, there were spiritual legalities to wipe out Israel as the law had established: an eye for an eye, and a tooth for a tooth.

Since the law does not save but condemns, we find the angel, who stood as the establishment of the written law, on Sinai with Moshe, demanding the just recompense of the law. It was the superiority of the testimony of Christ in Moshe that gave him the grace and authority to turn the angel of YHVH's presence from his wrath. Moses' life was a played out message and a prophetic life testifying of the Christ who was to come (Deuteronomy 18:15).

We see this same scenario with Jesus on Golgotha as our Lord appeased the demands of the law. He blotted out the handwriting that stood against us, elevating mankind from the domain of servanthood to sons. Jesus, through the cross, positionally set us above the elemental spirits of the universe. This He did by revealing the Father and bringing us into a conscious experience with His love.

The Father was never revealed until Jesus stepped on the earth, for no one knows the Father except the Son, and He alone reveals the Father. I believe that the law was also given to keep Israel away from the inheritance of sons, which comes through walking in the way of the tree of life. This is the path that YHVH instructed the cherubim to guard when He drove Adam out.

*"So he drove out the man and he placed Cherubim and a flaming sword which turned every way, at the east of the garden of Eden, to keep the **way of** the tree of life." (Genesis 3:24)*

The scripture says the *"way of,"* rather than the commonly accepted, *"way to."* The *"way of"* speaks of a lifestyle, a nature, a character. The *"way to"* is more directional. Thus, the way of the tree of life can be called "the mystical lifestyle to sonship." It leads to the partaking of the Tree of Life Himself. To do so is to partake of the nature of the Son. This is union that leads to the maturing of the sons.

The way was a lifestyle of journeying into oneness with Yeshua, guarded by the cherubim and a flaming sword, as it could only be revealed by the ultimate Son. Jesus alone could and can yield the flaming sword. This *mystical lifestyle of the tree of life* could only be walked by sons who have their seat of governance between the cherubim. Mankind had to be elevated from the domain of servanthood into the realm of sonship in order to be seated upon the cherubim. Remember, as mentioned before, our seat of governance is in Christ upon the cherubim.

"And hath raised us up together, and made us sit together in heavenly places in Christ Jesus." (Ephesians 2:6)

The law was our custodian that revealed the futility of our self-made righteousness to attain sonship. This self-effort is rooted in an orphan or servant mentality. The message of servants to receive acceptance through works could only be spoken by servants (angels), hence, the elemental spirits of the cosmos. The Jews clearly knew of their submission to YHVH through high angelic beings, or elemental spirits of the cosmos. Flavius Josephus, in his *Antiquities of the Jews*, wrote,

"We have learned the noblest of our doctrines and the holiest of our laws from the **angels** *sent by God."* (1 *Antiquities XV:136, or XV,5:3, Whiston's translation*)

The great Saint Paul also says,

"For if the word spoken by angels was steadfast, and every transgression and disobedience received a just recompense of reward." (Hebrews 2:2)

Sonship is revealed by sons. It is not because God did not want sons, but the fullness of time had not yet come for Jesus, the firstborn Son, Who is the revelation of sons to come. Therefore, YHVH ordained angels, who guarded this mystical path. These are the elementary spirits of the universe, mighty angelic beings who have different roles and functions in the cosmos. They had a close relationship with Moses.

Chapter 16

Lucifer: The Fallen Light Bearer

"*How art thou fallen from heaven, O Lucifer, son of the morning! how art thou cut down to the ground, which didst weaken the nations! For thou hast said in thine heart, I will ascend into heaven, I will exalt my throne above the stars of God: I will sit also upon the mount of the congregation, in the sides of the north: I will ascend above the heights of the clouds; I will be like the most High: Yet thou shalt be brought down to hell, to the sides of the pit.*" *(Isaiah 14:12-14)*

There is a lot of mystery concerning the history of this once beautiful cherubim. There is truth mixed with fables, speculations, and high imaginations, influenced by cultures and oral traditions. Where do we start when talking about a being that has plagued this cosmos for eons of time? A being whose history surpasses that of the earth? What really was his task, and from whence was iniquity found in him? This is one of the amazing files on angels I have been allowed to look into, the fall of this former light bearer.

Lucifer was once a glorious cherubim, whose Hebrew name is transliterated "*heylel.*" He was a shining one, a light bearer and bringer, as his name "*heylel,*" denotes. This cherubim was wonderfully clothed by the Light of Christ and his beauty was the emanation of Jesus' light. He was a mighty being, with a mighty task, which was to be a custodian of the pre-Adamic world. He brought the different spectrums of the light of Christ to creation.

God had assigned to him sanctuaries of this earthly cosmos as his sphere of influence. He was the being that was tasked to reveal the nature of YHVH to the pre-Adamic race, but he traded and defiled his realm of functionality. Iniquity was eventually found in him. Ezekiel writes this of him:

"*Thou wast perfect in thy ways from the day that thou wast created, till iniquity was found in thee. By the multitude of thy merchandise they have filled the midst of thee with violence, and thou hast sinned: therefore I will cast thee as profane out of the mountain of God: and I will destroy thee, O covering cherub, from the midst of the stones of fire. Thine heart was lifted up because of thy beauty, thou hast corrupted thy wisdom by reason of thy brightness: I will cast thee to the ground, I will lay thee before kings, that they may behold thee. Thou hast defiled thy sanctuaries by the multitude of thine iniquities, by the iniquity of thy traffick;*

therefore will I bring forth a fire from the midst of thee, it shall devour thee, and I will bring thee to ashes upon the earth in the sight of all them that behold thee." (Ezekiel 28:16-18)

As much as the defiling of his sanctuaries has to do with his nature, it is also concerned with his defiling of the earthly sanctuaries of which he was in charge. It was through iniquity that this happened.

Iniquity is the twisting of one's DNA such that one resonates and lives in response to the altered DNA. The DNA of heaven is the Light of Jesus Christ, and within His light is the nature and essence of YHVH. Lucifer, because of his pride, craved significance so much that he subtly twisted heaven's light to achieve this "honor" from the world. This pre-Adamic world's consciousness of YHVH eventually became twisted, so YHVH was viewed from a twisted light. The revelations of YHVH pulsating in that first earth carried within itself essences and filters of this cherub. This is one of the reasons that we are compelled to die completely to self.

I had a vision a few years ago while speaking at a small meeting in Toronto. In the vision, I saw myself standing in front of an open gate preaching to a crowd in front of me, and behind me was the Lord, gloriously adorned in a white light. I realized that I was blocking the revealing of His person as self was still standing in the way. I understood that as much as I was standing in front of the gate, I was also the gate. The gate had to be completely free from any self-imposed image of Michael to let the King come through.

When a man's heart begins to be lifted up in the quest of achieving notoriety or significance, he is entering and trading into a luciferian nature. This is what Satan did to the first pre-Adamic world. He blocked the light of Christ and reflected his nature by enforcing his will. He twisted heaven's light in order to be seen as something he is not. In doing so, he created Satan. The enemy lied and his lies were carried throughout the consciousness of the world. This was how iniquity was found in Him before Adam.

YHVH purged this world from the influence of the fallen cherubim through waters, which is why in Genesis 1, the earth is encompassed by waters. The flood of Noah was the second "waters" to purge this earth.

One of the stories I grew up hearing about the enemy was how he tried to take over the throne of God and oust God from heaven. This is not true, as the enemy's desire was for a position next to YHVH. Lucifer knew that to take over the throne of God, he would have to be God, and he knew perfectly well that this was impossible. What he wanted was to be as God; not replace God. Being like God is a state of being seated in a place meant for sons of YHVH, conformed into the image and likeness of Jesus. If you'll notice, the enemy's heart's desire as outlined by Isaiah is to be *"like the Most High."* He never said, *"I will be the Most High."* He said,

*"I will ascend above the heights of the clouds; I will be **like** the most High."* *(Isaiah 14:12)*

The enemy desired the position of sonship, co-ruling and co-reigning with YHVH. This is why he hates sonship. Sonship in and through Jesus Christ positionally and experientially elevates us above the domain and governance of any being, whether they are thrones, dominions, or powers. The battle between the forces of darkness and us is all for a living realm called sonship.

For further clarity, let us look at how war broke out in Heaven.

"And there appeared another wonder in heaven; and behold a great red dragon, having seven heads and ten horns, and seven crowns upon his heads. And his tail drew the third part of the stars of heaven, and did cast them to the earth: and the dragon stood before the woman which was ready to be delivered, for to devour her child as soon as it was born." (Revelation 12:3-4)

The woman in Revelations 12 brought forth a Man-Child. Notice, the enemy's battle is with the Child. The Child represents the seed of Jesus Christ, which is you and me. So the devil conducts a long standing vendetta that if he cannot be like the Most High, then mankind cannot be like the Most High. So his fight is that we would not be conformed into the image of God. If we cannot look like our Father, we cannot function as His sons.

As we bear the image of the earthly, it's time we bear the image of the heavenly DNA of Jesus Christ. This can only be achieved through divine union with the Son of God.

Chapter 17

The Serpent, the Tree of Knowledge, and the Earth

W orking with angels means interacting and flowing within the dimension of heaven. To fully experience the dimension of heaven, we need to rise above our earthly influence. This requires understanding why the earth was made. We need to know how one might end up being tied within the earth's frequencies. We must also know about the tree of the knowledge of good and evil, since its consciousness resulted in angels falling and operating within the earthly metacosm. Before we tackle all this, let us briefly look at some of the reasons the earth was formed.

The Earth

It was the Holy Spirit who said to John G. Lake,

"For the earth is a school to prepare thee for glory; the lessons here learnt , you will always obey. When eternity dawns, it will be only the morning of life with me always, as life is today. Therefore, be not impatient, as lessons thou'rt learning; each day will bring gladness and joy to thee here;but Heaven will reveal to thy soul, of the treasure which infinitude offers, through ages and years. For thy God is the God of the earth and the heavens; and thy soul is the soul that He died to save, and His blood is sufficient, His power eternal; therefore rest in thy God, both today and always." (John G. Lake : The complete collection of his life teachings, Compiled by Roberts Liardon, pg 737)

The world and its system is not the same as the earth. Our earth was created as a womb, a learning facility which brings forth the fruit of the consciousness of its custodian. The world, on the other hand, is a physical domain framed from the consciousness and influence of the enemy. It is the manifestation of the nature of fallen spirit beings, empowered and expressed through the tree of the knowledge of good and evil. The current worldly systems since Adam have belonged to the enemy. Our father Adam gave them over, and this is the reason we are not of the world. This is the difference between the world and the earth; the earth has always been the Lord's and the fulness thereof (Psalm 24:1).

The original intent of this "womb" we call earth was to birth forth the consciousness of the sons of God and also to be a teaching facility, but this did not play out as YHVH ordained. Adam relinquished his right to frame a world of YHVH to the enemy.

God created the cosmos, other worlds and planets both inhabited and uninhabited. He made our earth the center, the hub, and the headquarters of the infinite continuous revelations of God through the person of our Lord Jesus Christ. The inhabitants of this planet were to venture into other planets and worlds to bring the revelation of God through experiential knowledge of Him. This, in turn, would cause all of creation to understand and come in line with their preordained purposes.

The destinies and goals of all created things, seen or unseen, whether they be thrones, dominions, powers, stars, planets, molecules and atoms, the created universes, both spiritual and physical, is in correspondence to their revelation of YHVH. The revelation of YHVH is found in the person of Jesus Christ.

The scriptures tell us that creation is groaning for the manifestation of the sons of God. This is because through the manifestation of the sons of God, the unparalleled revelation of YHVH flows to all creation, unveiling and revealing the true nature of all created things.

The earth was made to be part of the cosmos wherein the revelation of YHVH was to be brought forth through His sons who are in divine union with Him. It is the reflection of God in the face of Jesus Christ that brings order to all creation.

How was this formulated by YHVH? God dwells in the heavens, which is a spiritual dimension. Eden was created and existed as part of the undefiled "*astral plane*" of the universe; thus, it was a bridge between two worlds. It acted as a perfect soul realm of creation. The earth, on the other hand, was a physical aspect. This was the original form of the spirit, soul, and body of the earth.

Eden bridged the physical and spiritual dimensions through being a realm of the pleasures of YHVH. For Adam to bring the realities of heaven into the earth, he had to go through the "ecstasies and pleasures" of YHVH. For him to ascend and bring the experiential knowledge of God to all creation, he had to enjoy the living God. God greatly desired that our knowledge and lessons of Him learned would be administered to all creation through the gateway of pleasure, which was Eden.

The Serpent and the Tree of the Knowledge of Good and Evil

"Now the serpent was more subtil than any beast of the field which the LORD God had made. And he said unto the woman, Yea, hath God said, Ye shall not eat of every tree of the garden?" (Genesis 3:1)

"And the great dragon was cast out, that old serpent, called the Devil, and Satan, which deceiveth the whole world: he was cast out into the earth, and his angels were cast out with him." (Revelation 12:9)

"He seized the dragon, that ancient serpent who is the Devil and Satan, and bound him for 1,000 years." (Revelation 20:2)

How does a serpent, a being synonymous with Lucifer (Revelation 20:22), find himself freely roaming within God's garden? What legalities did he have to be a custodian of the tree of the knowledge of good and evil? Would God in all His goodness put death within the reach of his children, if death didn't have a legal right to be there?

Death existed prior to Adam, looking for a landing pad. Adam was that channel, which introduced death into creation, manifested through partaking of the consciousness of the tree of the knowledge of good and evil.

The tree of the knowledge of good and evil was the consciousness that Lucifer traded into the angels that eventually fell. It is a factor that reasons and questions YHVH's perfection, goodness, and truth. It is that consciousness of death that makes one think that in God, there is room to bypass His will and make Him compromise. The tree of the knowledge of good and evil is also the subtle desire to be like the Most High apart from Him. Anything done apart from the leading and touch of YHVH will always strip you from His essence and His nature. We cannot be like God apart from God. There is nothing as Luciferian to the core as trying to attain sonship apart from the ultimate Son, Jesus. His light is the garment of sonship. The tree of good and evil is a mixture of light and darkness. But how does darkness form from within light?

The origin of darkness stems from a spirit being's negative inward perspective of YHVH's nature. It springs up from within the consciousness of spirit beings who have begun to question YHVH"s doings. Darkness is light, but it is a different form of light. Our Lord Jesus Christ, the source of light, clearly showed this when He said,

"Take heed therefore that the light which is in thee be not darkness." (Luke 11:35)

Darkness is light that has been tampered with to the point that it now radiates the raw identity of the being who carries it and not the identity of the Father of Lights. Since it no longer radiates the glories of its origin, who is Jesus, it neither carries the essences of life nor divine revelations of Christ. Hence, it brings death.

Since darkness is twisted light, it is energy, but unlike that of Christ, this type of energy is destructive. It is this energy that the enemy uses to advance his kingdom. It is also this energy that the spirit of self-promoting, self-seeking ministries use to achieve their goals which are not inspired by the living Christ. Again, I say, there is nothing as satanic to the core as trying to use Christ's light for self-worth and recognition, even if the motive is good. This will only result in creating darkness in oneself.

God made all spirit beings by His light, and the moment we, as spirit beings, begin to question His light, we create ripples of darkness within us. The questioning is more like reasoning and measuring His goodness. This was the origin of Satan's demise. Isaiah records,

"For thou hast said in thine heart, I will ascend into heaven, I will exalt my throne above the stars of God: I will sit also upon the mount of the congregation, in the sides of the north." (Isaiah 14:13)

The darkness of the rebellious nature of Lucifer began in his heart. It was in the faculty of his thoughts and patterns, questioning YHVH's goodness. He reasoned, "If God is truly the embodiment of goodness, why am I not up there, co-ruling with Him?" This was pride taking root and translating itself in his consciousness.

Pride reveals itself as a subtle desire for a place of authority or position that YHVH has not assigned for you. It is also copy-catting the nature and flow of another spirit other than Jesus. Losing your God-given uniqueness and coveting to be like another, either in ministry or otherwise, is rooted in pride. How so? Because when one enters this terrain, the heart is saying, " I am better. I deserve a better position of authority. Why did God give me this one? I should be like so and so."

This was the fall of Lucifer, pride taking root within him, birthing the consciousness of the tree of the knowledge of good and evil. This consciousness, when it had fully matured as a tree, was fed and traded into other angels, who eventually joined in the rebellion. Angels partook of an ungodly tree and fell. The tree is synonymous with the presence and workings of Lucifer, for it was a manifestation of his consciousness; hence, wherever Lucifer is, it is found. It is the devil's power of influence, his self-styled way of attaining God-likeness, a failed promise he gave to angels and Adam.

The first place that found deliverance from the influence of this tree was heaven when the devil and his angels were cast out. Since the enemy was not locked up or cast into the abyss, which I believe was one of Adam's tasks, he had a legal right to have his consciousness within Eden, manifested as a tree.

A tree yields fruit, and by eating of it, one partakes of its nature. Since the tree was within the earth's dimension, its partaker and custodian had to carry the frequencies of earth. As Adam was the image of the invisible God, the serpent was Lucifer's physical expression on this earth, and he was more subtle than all the beasts of the field.* He is referred to as a beast of the field, because he was made from the elements and substance of the earth. The serpent, though created by God, was put into the garden through spiritual legalities.

154

The ancient serpent was first cast out of heaven to the earth, in order to be cast from the earth into Hades. As Michael (who is like God) cast Satan out of heaven, Adam (the one who is like God, by virtue of being made in the image of God) was supposed to cast the enemy out and uproot the tree out of the garden. When the serpent managed to deceive Eve, the Lord sentenced the serpent:

"And the LORD God said unto the serpent, Because thou hast done this, thou art cursed above all cattle, and above every beast of the field; upon thy belly shalt thou go, and dust shalt thou eat all the days of thy life." (Genesis 3:14)

Let us look at YHVH's first judgement on the enemy, *"upon thy belly shalt thou go, and dust of the field shalt thou eat"* (Genesis 3:14). I believe this has to do with tying and limiting the serpent's influence within the frequencies of the earthly cosmos, signified through the dust of the earth. Satan's rule, influence, and authority can only go as far as the earthly metacosm. That old serpent is tied to this earth realm, and because of this, his main objective is to try to confine the spirit of man within the fallen degenerative earthly metacosm.

"And I heard a loud voice saying in heaven, Now is come salvation, and strength, and the kingdom of our God, and the power of his Christ: for the accuser of our brethren is cast down, which accused them before our God day and night. And they overcame him by the blood of the Lamb, and by the word of their testimony; and they loved not their lives unto the death. Therefore rejoice, ye heavens, and ye that dwell in them. Woe to the inhabiters of the earth and of the sea! for the devil is come down unto you, having great wrath, because he knoweth that he hath but a short time. And when the dragon saw that he was cast unto the earth, he persecuted the woman which brought forth the man child." (Revelation 12:10-13)

John of Patmos saw the expulsion of the enemy from heaven. Notice how John clearly records that the enemy was "cast" to the earth. The "casting" is more than a hurling of Lucifer to the earth realm, but it also means confining his influence to the atmospheres that surround our earthly metacosm. Our earthly metacosm is the realm that constitutes the first and second heavens. John goes on to record the voice that urges the inhabitants of heaven to "rejoice." Rejoicing is meant for heavenly dwellers, and these are those who have consciously pursued oneness with Yeshua, for they are with Him where He is.

Only by fully making heaven our abode and understanding that Jesus came and *"...through him, we both have access by one Spirit unto the Father and therefore are no more strangers and foreigners, but fellow citizens with the saints, and of the household of God"* (Ephesians 2:18-19) can we truly partake of the essences of heaven. Heaven is not some mystical place that the saints go to when they die. It is the basis from which we function. We are to terraform this earthly metacosm from heaven to earth.

The fallen angels' desires, inspired and lead by the serpent, act as a barrier between heaven and earth. By virtue of their corrupted nature, they try to prevent the free flow from heaven to earth and from earth to heaven. In order for us not to be under the serpent's domain, we have to be seated above him.

We have authority over something to the degree that we are seated above it. This should not just be a knowledge of our positional seating that has been wrought in Christ Jesus, but the reality of experiencing the heavenly places. If we consciously submit to the earth's frequencies, we are dishonoring the death and resurrection of Jesus. Jesus died, rose, and has elevated us into heavenly places. He snatched us from the earthly consciousness and frequencies so that we can be fellow citizens and partakers of heavenly frequencies and consciousness.

The earth devours and houses its own kind, those who still vibrate and strongly resemble the frequency of the earth. They find their sustenance from partaking of the tree of the knowledge of good and evil. The spiritual consciousness from the tree of the knowledge of good and evil callously numbs men's perceptibility of a higher spiritual universe. It positionally places man under the domain and rule of the serpent; thus, those who are under the influence of the tree of the knowledge have no perception of God, as God can only be seen and experienced in the heavenly dimensions.

Men who partake of this tree can never navigate the realms of heaven, but are solely limited to the astral plane, a domain under the influence of the serpent and fallen angels. Jesus has purposed His Church to be transdimensional and explorers of the heavenly universes. The heavenly realm is the domain and operation of the Church.

Chapter 18

A Glimpse into Spiritual Growth and Angels

Our growth in the Lord brings with it an increased unveiling of our purposes. This increased revelation of who we are in Him also means knowing Him in an intimate way, and those who know Him perform exploits (Daniel 11:32). Exploits always involve and include angelic aid, which means that the angels around us also come into their full active roles in our lives as we grow into the Lord. Becoming spiritually mature enables us to walk in more authority, thus engaging and instructing further angelic help and intervention. Let us remember,

*"For the **spirits** of the prophets are subject to the prophets." (1 Corinthians 14:32)*

The word "subject" in this verse implies that the *"spirits"* of the prophet are in a parallel perpetual dependence on the prophet, but it is a dependence of servitude and a non-violation of the prophets' will, whose will should always be in alignment with the Lord's. This truth has to be literally played out, and it can only be demonstrated if the inner us, the spirit man, which is our raw identity, takes rulership and government of our entire faculties. Thus, our entire being enters into divine identity. When we resonate in who we truly are in Jesus, we can instruct and mobilize the spirits that are subject to us through God's grace. Lest we forget, the spirits here that Paul was referring to were not the Holy Spirit, neither is it our spirit man. Paul was referring to angels, which he calls *ministering spirits* in Hebrews 1:14.

The prophet is subject to the Holy Spirit. The angels are subject to the prophets. The whole spiritual universe of Yeshua is subject to the Lord.

Faith

The author of Hebrews quotes the great exploits of "normal" men like us, who shaped history and terraformed this cosmos with the aroma and beauty of heaven simply because they believed. Great angelic intervention and help was initiated by these men because of their faith. To them, they had perceived and understood the branches of the tree of faith. One of the most important of these branches to the angelic canopy is the branch of its sound and voice. Our faith has a sound and a voice.

"Is He, therefore, who gives The Spirit among you, and does miracles among you, of the works of The Written Law, or of the HEARING OF FAITH?" (Galatians 3:1,2,5, Aramaic Version)

Paul shows clearly and demonstrates to the Galatians that the Lord is doing miracles among them through the *sound* of their faith. Notice, the phrase *"the hearing of faith,"* meaning that faith releases a sound. This sound or voice is one which the angels adhere and attend to.

The vibrational frequency of the sound of faith, proceeding from the heart of an individual, is embedded in the genetic makeup and structure of an angel. Faith is like a sound wave. It sends out a signal which activates a response from the angelic hosts to bring to pass that which the individual was believing God for. We have the capacity to initiate angelic activity through the sound and the voice of faith. The sound of our faith has to be amplified enough to the point wherein it proceeds from our hearts at a higher frequency which angels can heed. How, then, is my faith amplified?

The only way the sound and voice of our faith can be amplified is through love. This means that we also love the angels that the Lord of the Angel Armies has made available for the sons of God. Faith works and is energized and empowered by love. To fully understand how important the amplification of our faith is, we need to look at Abraham, who I will also call "the man of love." Faith is energized by love. Abraham believed God because he had a love relationship with God. It is this love that solidified a steadfast faith in Abraham, who had powerful encounters with the angels.

It was through this faith that Abraham saw and heard the cry for his descendants to have a resting place. His faith had the power to take him into a day where he saw that it is only through the sacrifice of Yeshua that men can be ushered into the living City.

So by faith, Abraham intimately held his descendants within his heart, and the love which he had for them emitted powerful vibrational frequencies which amplified the sound of his faith. This caused the angels to respond by framing a city which became a tangible reality called Abraham's Bosom. Abraham's Bosom was an expression of his heart's desire for a temporary resting place for his descendants.

Love energizes faith. Faith produces a sound or a voice that is well-crafted and designed to merge into an angel's spiritual makeup. This activates the angels to carry out their specified assignments.

Love - Heaven's Language

"For even the Son of man came not to be ministered unto, but to minister, and to give his life a ransom for many." (Mark 10:45)

The principle of love is the principle upon which the angelic canopy rests. Yeshua came to minister and to serve, which is love in action. Angels are ministering spirits which flow and minister from a position of love. Every angelic act, touch, feeling, gesture, or glimpse is the manifestation of the Father's love to us and for us. Angels are messengers of love. The fact that they are present right now with you as you are reading this is because the Father has spoken over you, "I love you My beloved child. I have loved you with an everlasting love."

This spoken word is the love song of YHVH over you, which has fused itself into the genetic makeup and structure of the angels. Angelic movement and involvement in your life are a communication of the Father's love. You have angelic help not only because you are a son, but because you are loved. That is why there is constant angelic ministering throughout the earth for Christians, non-Christians, atheists, and others.

"For God so loved the world..." (John 3:16)

We can all attest to stories of those who are not of the Christian faith, yet they have some sort of angelic intervention. This help is initiated by the constant love of the Father over all. God's love is like the sun which rises over all, awaiting mankind to bask in its rays. The rays of His love choreographs angelic help to the world.

The Holy Spirit has lavishly shed the love of God in our hearts (as Christians) and His love in us is not meant to be caged, but we are to emanate it to the world. The rays of His love flowing from our hearts initiates and triggers angelic intervention. As He is, so are we (1 John 4:17). We have the God-given capacity to love a nation and initiate angelic help to the masses.

In every revival, there is massive angelic activity which is increased and energized through love.Therefore, a baptism of love is the prelude to revivals. True revivalists are those who have learned to love. This is the love we are all to be known by. To emphasize my former statement; there are two types of angelic activities: one that is initiated solely by God, and the other, that you and I can personally initiate. The first one is solely as a result of the Father's love for humanity. The second is as a result of our love, which energizes the frequency and power of our faith.

Jesus came to bring many sons unto glory. Sonship is the progressive manifestation of the ultimate Son Jesus Christ, in and through us, who did all He did from the foundation of love. Jesus' entry into this cosmos was born of the unstoppable love of God, He who is the author of all things, knitted creation together in love.

"And, having made peace through the blood of his cross, by him to reconcile all things unto Himself; by Him, I say, whether they be things in earth, or things in heaven." (Colossians 1:20)

The ultimate Son came to cause all things in heaven and earth to co-exist together in harmony. He bridged the invisible and the visible realms by love. *Love is the doorway into infinite angelic activities and encounters.* God poured the streams of liquid love into this cosmos, which is awaiting our response: to fully love Him who first loved us. Being lovers of God establishes the bridge between the visible and invisible realms. This is the bridge upon which angels travel to and fro.

One of the sad things that has plagued the body of Christ is our misconception of love. True, genuine love, which knitted together the early church, is missing. Many have fallen into the deception of "niceness;" wherein we view love as an act of "niceness," we have also somehow bound ourselves with *"soulish rights."* As long as we feel like have rights, we are not walking in love. The cross is the place where we die to all our rights and wants, the place where we continually learn to identify ourselves with our brothers until we see no difference between them and us. "By this (love) shall all men know that you are my disciples."

The angelic canopy cannot be fooled. Genuine love needs to be the root of all our acts and endeavors. The simple manifestation of the angels, their touch and influence in our lives through the person of the Holy Spirit, is to raise the consciousness of our souls into the realms of the Father's love.

Final Thoughts

I remember one evening when I was spending time with the Lord. Suddenly, I became overwhelmed by a great sense of His beauty and love. The magnificence of His face so enveloped me that I spontaneously uttered, "That I may be for your love."

Inebriated by His beauty, I looked to my right and noticed that I had a visitor. A glorious angel was standing a few feet from me, dressed in pure gold armor like a medieval knight. It seemed to me as if the gold signified the purity of the King's love, love that even in thick darkness shines as daylight.

The angel carried a sharp golden spear and I wondered if he had come to wound me completely for the King's love. With a tender, yet powerful voice, the angel said, "My name is, 'For-His-Love.'" His persona and the golden armor were so inviting and magnificent. The angel went on to say, "The greatest honor we (angels) have is for the King's lovers. And you have purposed in your heart to attain one thing, 'To be for His Love,' and for that same reason am I sent to you."

The truth is that we all want supernatural experiences, and some of us want the excitement of the experiences without a lover's commitment. It will not and cannot work, as all of creation longs for His loving goodness. Only true lovers of Jesus can minister His love.

Creation will respond to sons of YHVH who are the image of love. Our mandate is to bring all creation into the conscious experience of the love of the Son. Angels desire to minister to lovers of Jesus. Fall in love with Jesus and let everything flow from there.

ABOUT THE AUTHOR

Michael Aviel experienced a radical encounter with Jesus in 2009 when he was born again in the liquid love of Jesus Christ. What began as conversations between him and the Lord is now put together in book form to share some of the things that God has revealed to him about the angelic community of the Kingdom of light.

He is passionate about engaging the kingdom of God within us to behold and savour the beauty of Jesus Christ - "the simplicity of turning inwards to behold the beauty of Yeshua".

His heart is to help others to know that through a deep, loving relationship with Jesus Christ, we can and should engage with the angels of Yahovah Sabaoth.

Michael lives in Toronto, Canada where he is a senior leader at Ecclesia of Burning Ones. He speaks at various gatherings, co-host conferences and a conference speaker.

Made in the USA
Columbia, SC
22 March 2019